PRAISE FOR H
HOW TO DISCO

C000220862

ENTREPRENEURIAL MOJO

"Passion is great. Purpose is fantastic. The thing is, if you don't have action in place, nothing happens. Author Pat Duckworth created this resource so you can take strategic action. Her no-nonsense approach to shifting your behavior is refreshing."

Dr. Shawne Duperon, Six Time EMMY® winner, Project: Forgive Founder

"Sometimes books give you theory or motivation. This book gives you both. I really enjoyed the neurological underpinnings outlined to empower you to create an aligned and congruent path in life. Relevant stories from women entrepreneurs also helped to cement the concepts. Thought-provoking read."

Lisa Mininni, President, Excellerate Associates, Best-Selling Author, *Me, Myself, and Why? The Secrets to Navigating Change*

"Pat Duckworth's book *Hot Women Rock* is exactly what our society needs today! 23% of all new entrepreneurs are between the ages of 50 and 65 and who better than a woman with experience to create the heart based changes necessary to lead our world through the 21st century. By

following Pat and her guests' examples, I have no doubt a successful business awaits those that embrace the teachings found in *Hot Women Rock.*"

Frank Moffatt, CEO and Founder of Your Second Fifty

"I love this book!! It's a must read for midlife entrepreneurs. It's not just about setting up a business, but rather how to dive deep and use your inner resources to create success living your life's purpose. I literally couldn't stop reading the second part of the book filled with true stories from real women who overcame tremendous challenges and emerged triumphant in their chosen careers."

Debra Poneman, Best-Selling Author and Co-Founder of *Your Year of Miracles mentoring program for women*

"Pat Duckworth provides rich information that entrepreneurials need to know but her thought-provoking questions and exercises causes you to really go deep within yourself which ensures your success whether you are a new entrepreneur or one who has been in business for years."

Wendy Woodworth, Calgary. Dance With Life Again

"If you have the desire to create and manage your own company during your second fifty, *Hot Women Rock* is the book that encourages you, proves you can do it, and gets you started.

In the first half of the book, author Pat Duckworth shows you how. The exercises within are infectious allowing the mind to imagine the possibilities, yet offers the structure to focus on what is most important.

The second half of the book shares the wins and challenges of several female entrepreneurs who started business in their second 50. *Hot Women Rock* proves that it is never too late to pursue your dream, use the right tools to stay focused, and that no obstacle is too big.

Now, it's your turn. What's your story?"

Catherine Saykaly-Stevens, Author and Speaker, *The Networking Web*

"Years ago I asked my mother, "Why do they call menopause the "change of life", anyway?" My mother replied, "Because it's when you realize you need to change your life!" Pat Duckworth has written the road map to navigate that process of change for every woman who wants to explore a new, entrepreneurial journey. I love the whole person approach that Pat uses and the exercises in this book are a must if you want to create lasting change."

Tina Dietz MS, NCC, Founder, Start Something Creative Business Solutions, International Best-Selling author and speaker

"I SO wish I had had *Hot Women Rock* when I started my first business—it would have saved me a lot of headache. If you're a woman wi—ser than 50 with an unfulfilled passion for being an entrepreneur, this book will have you on the way to the business of your dreams before you know it. It is NEVER too late!"

Nancy Ogilvie, Our Climate Change Legacy

"So many women are feeling a pull in the second half of their lives to create a life that tantalizes and fulfills. This book takes them by the hand and shows them exactly how they can do this. I loved the exercises, which even if one decided not to become an entrepreneur are the kind of tasks that highlight important things about who you are.

Pat Duckworth rounds it off nicely by including personal stories that create a picture of how things might look in real-life."

Debbie Pokornik, Award winning author of *Standing in Your Power and Break Free of Parenting Pressures*

"If you are a mature woman seeking a one stop guide for reinventing yourself, look no further. In Hot Women Rock: How to Discover your Midlife Entrepreneurial Mojo, Pat Duckworth draws on her extensive background in NLP, Cognitive Hypnotherapy, and business to offer a clear, concise roadmap for clarifying your purpose to create a new powerful, authentic, and rewarding entrepreneurial career. Fledgling and seasoned entrepreneurs alike will find nuggets of wisdom in this excellent guide and reference book. Richly illustrated with true stories from a variety of successful women who embraced new careers later in life, as well as insightful exercises, and a plethora of resources Hot Women is undeniably a winner! "Hot Woman" Pat Duckworth has rocked it out of the park again with her brilliant new book!"

MarBeth Dunn, Miracle Worker, Intuitive, Author, Speaker

"Pat Duckworth is simply brilliant. It is never too late to pursue your passion and this book will inspire you to take action now. The entrepreneurs' stories in Part 2 leave you with no excuses. These inspirational women have overcome personal and professional challenges to achieve great success and happiness. This book is a cutting-edge approach to the business of becoming an entrepreneur to pursue your life's purpose. If you've reached a point in your life where you want to make a difference and gain personal fulfilment this book is for you."

Teresa de Grosbois, #1 International Bestselling author of *Mass Influence*

"This book is a game changer for so many women around the world who have reached an age in life where they are forced to look inwards and explore what it means to live a fulfilled life. If you are one of these women, this is a pivotal point for you and this book is for you. Pat Duckworth is a larger than life visionary committed to birthing new life into millions of women and this book will show you what is possible when you follow your dreams and live a fulfilled life at any age."

Judy van Niekerk, Founder of The Digital Bra, Best-Selling Author & Philanthropist

If you ask me, "How much is a duck worth?" *A play on Pats last name I would say "priceless".* The information contained in this book is truly priceless. This book will save you years in your quest of what it is you want out of life!

Pat has done an incredible job of taking the complexity out of, "Who am I and what do I want to do with my life" and put it into concrete achievable and easy to follow steps. Which are usable not just by "Hot Women", but anyone searching for their entrepreneurial mojo.

L. Neil Thrussell B *Three time International Best Selling Author, Speaker, Facilitator, Life Coach*

HOT WOMEN ROCK

How to discover Your Midlife
Entrepreneurial Mojo

PAT DUCKWORTH

Published by

HWCS Publications
White House
Meeting Lane
Litlington
Royston, Cambs SG8 0QF
England

Max Caddick, Cover design
maxcaddick@hotmail.com

Philip S Marks, Editor

Ginger Marks, Layout
DocUmeantDesigns
www.DocUmeantDesigns.com

For inquiries about volume orders, contact the Publisher in writing.

ISBN-13: 978-0-9926620-2-8 (paperback)
ISBN-10: 0992662028

DEDICATION

To the wonderful women in my 'Secret Six Mastermind Group' just for being there.

CONTENTS

PART 2

ACKNOWLEDGEMENTS

Massive thanks to the *Hot Women Entrepreneurs* who have shared their stories with me and graciously offered their permission to share their stories in this book, in alphabetical order: Alessandra Alonso, Ann Bennett, Beverley Glick, Brenda Jacobson, Christine Powers, Deborah Granville, Dianna Bowes, Helen Rebello, Jill McCulloch, Karen Knott, Kay Newton, Kimberly Mylls, Lesley Pyne, Liberty Forrest, Marci Shimoff, Nancy Ogilvie, Pamela Thompson, Patricia McBride, Rhoberta Shaler, Sally Saunders-Makings, and Wendy Woodworth

Thank you to Teresa de Grobois and my wonderful friends in the Evolutionary Business Council who are such a support and inspiration.

I am grateful to Charmaine Hammond for the Foreword.

Liberty Forrest and Cemanthe McKenzie inspired the amazing book cover

Huge thanks to Sally Saunders-Makings of ESSE Retail and Oliver Makings of Caligraving Ltd for supporting my book launch.

FOREWORD

It's never too late to fulfil your life purpose.

Many women delay pursuing their dreams and bucket list items in the earlier part of their life while they set up a home, establish their career, and take care of a family.

Women working outside the home often choose to be employees to ensure a sense of financial and job security.

Later, at midlife, women experience many changes in their life contexts as well as in their physical bodies. For some women this is the trigger to make bigger changes to finally live their dreams and pursue their passions once put on hold. For others, a new sense of purpose may have developed. Becoming an entrepreneur may be part of that dream.

My own experience of transformation from working as a Correctional Officer and Supervisor at a Young Offender facility to becoming an entrepreneur and business owner and setting up my philanthropic projects such as our Million Acts of Kindness tours is one such example. Sometimes life's situations inspire the need for change or the inspiration to pursue a different path. That was my case . . . returning to university as an adult, I achieved an MA and now am celebrating almost 20 years of owning my own businesses as an author and global transformational speaker. A very different path than working in the Correctional System. There is however a common thread in my past and current path . . . the desire to make a difference, promote kindness/ acceptance and respect, and, have ongoing opportunities for creativity and challenges. Ultimately this is about living my purpose, fulfilling my goals and creating my best life. It is never too late to return to school . . . open a business. . . . Or pursue your dreams.

In Hot Women Rock, Pat is offering an approach to help you to align your mind set to turbo charge your entrepreneurial spirit.

Most books for entrepreneurs focus on the practical steps you need to take to set yourself up in business and start to market your product or process. In this book, Pat takes a step back and introduces you to a deeper approach. It starts with developing a profound understanding of what your purpose is. From the foundation of that understanding you can build towards taking exquisite, effective action. By aligning your mind-set you will have the strength to deal with the obstacles that arise between you and your dream.

When I met Pat at one of my global events I was struck by her enthusiasm for her midlife entrepreneurial journey. She impressed me with her energy and enthusiasm. She is always ready to learn and take action on what she has learned. I am certain that you will learn from this book and the inspirational women's stories contained in it. You too can achieve your life purpose.

Charmaine Hammond, MA, BA
Professional Speaker, Best-Selling author, and Founder Million Acts of Kindness tour

INTRODUCTION

Mid-life is a time of tremendous change in women's lives. You might be thinking of the physical changes that come with declining reproductive hormones; changes in body shape, hair colour, and skin tone. Or maybe you are thinking about the emotional changes; the rollercoaster of moods that are not unlike the teenage years.

The mid-life years can also be a time of great change in your personal life and circumstances. Children are becoming independent and leaving home, parents are getting older and may need support, and finances may be getting easier or harder.

Your relationship with your partner may be changing. Unfortunately, the statistics on divorce at midlife indicate that more relationships are ending among people in their 50s and 60s. The US National Centre for Health and Statistics reported a 16% increase in divorce rates for couples married 30 years or more.

While all this change is going on it can be the perfect time to make changes in your work-life. In the US, 23% of all new entrepreneurs are age 50-65, so you are not alone. The average age of the founders of US technology companies is 39, with twice as many over age 50 as under age 25.

According to the Office for National Statistics, there are now nearly 1.8 million self-employed people over the age of 50 in the UK, an increase of 21 per cent since 2008. Around one in five people aged over 50 is self-employed, a higher proportion than for any other age group. A survey by Age UK, the charity for older people, indicates that more than 70% of businesses started by people in their fifties survive for at least five years whereas only 28% of those started by younger people last that long.

The majority of workers over 50 want to continue working beyond state pension age, 62% of women and 59% of men. For some it is to supplement their income. In 2008 24% of men and 37% of women in the UK had incomes which were less than adequate with 20% of women and 6% of men claiming that their income is completely inadequate to meet their needs.

A significant number of older entrepreneurs set up business out of a sense of purpose. More on that later.

My story

I think I was born old-fashioned! I left school at 18 and went straight to work because I wanted financial independence. University seemed like an indulgence. I have a strong public service ethic, inherited from my parents, so I went to work for a local authority in London. There I trained to be a Chartered Surveyor.

Over the next 32 years I worked in the public and voluntary sector, progressing from technical work to management, and finally to corporate roles. By the time I was 50 years of age I had an MBA and I had risen to the dizzy heights of being a Deputy Director in the Senior Civil Service. Everything I had worked for and aspired to.

You can guess what comes next. I wasn't happy. The view from my pinnacle was not as good as I thought it would be. I was commuting to and from London for 3 hours every day. I was working long hours. My boss didn't respect or value my skills. That voice in my head that had been saying "What are you going to do when you grow up?" was getting louder and louder.

One morning I was walking through the park on the way to the office and I became aware that there were tears running down my cheeks. That voice in my head said, "Life is too short to be miserable. It's time to make a change."

I had been interested in complementary therapies for years. I had encouraged my mother to train to be a reflexologist when she was 70! A friend had introduced me to Neuro Linguistic Programming (NLP) in the 1980s and I had been thinking about studying it but I was too busy with work and family. It was time to take action.

So I signed up for a ten month Cognitive Hypnotherapy course. I had no idea how I was going to cope with the weekend a month on the course plus any homework and studying, but the universe rewards action. No sooner had I committed to the course than a scheme came up at work to take early retirement. Result.

My husband has always been supportive and that is a huge benefit. I rushed home and told him about the scheme and, without hesitation, he said "Apply!" Six nail-biting weeks later my application was approved and my last day was set for 31 December. New year, new start.

1 January 2010 was the start of my entrepreneurial journey. I had lots of transferable skills that I had learned in the public sector and a treasury of life experiences to draw from. I knew next to nothing about running a business but my attitude was all about learning, developing, and enjoying my new life.

In the next five years I set up in practice, delivered courses and workshops, wrote three books, developed five online programs, and was on stage as a speaker in the UK, Canada, and Cyprus. This year I have already been to San Diego and spoken on stage in India for the first time. I know, I can't believe it either!

Supercharge your mojo

I don't just want to share with you what I have learned, I want to inspire you to take the first steps towards your new life. There is a Neuro-Linguistic Programming (NLP) model that is so powerful that it makes a difference to everyone that I teach it to. This book is based on that model.

I am going to talk you through the practical application of the model of Neurological Levels, which I will call NLLs from this point forward, and how it can supercharge your entrepreneurial mojo.

You can read this book as I've written it from the top level NLL (Purpose) to the lowest (Environment) or you can read the chapters in the opposite order. If you are a blue sky thinker who likes to understand the concepts, you will probably prefer to start at the beginning. If you are a woman who likes to know the details and the step by step process, you will probably prefer to start at the end and work backwards. It is your choice.

The important thing is that you read all of the chapters. As I will explain, aligning your NLLs will give you a strength and authenticity like nothing else you have experienced. With that strength comes success, enjoyment, and fulfil-ment. You don't want to spend this stage of your life doing something you don't enjoy.

I have also included some inspirational entrepreneurial women's stories. These are all real life stories that have been told to me to help to inspire you. All of these women had challenges and problems they had to overcome, just as you will. They have all started with a different purpose and defined success in different ways. You can learn from how they kept going and achieved so much in their midlife. I feel privileged to know them.

Trouble shooting

What this book isn't is a step by step guide to setting up in business. It is about developing the right mind-set. The Resources section at the end of the book provides more practical guidance.

Part 1

FINDING STRENGTH THROUGH YOUR AUTHENTICITY

"Walt Disney told his crew to "build the castle first" when construct-ing Disney World, knowing that it would continue to serve as moti-vation throughout the project. Oftentimes when people fail to achieve what they want in life, it's because their vision isn't strong enough."
—*Gail Blanke, President and CEO, Lifedesigns*

The concept of Neurological Levels started with the anthro-pologist Gregory Bateson. He suggested that the logical processes of the brain are organised into different levels or hierarchies. Changes made at the highest neurological level will affect change at the lower levels whereas changes made at the lower levels may or may not affect the upper levels.

The way that I think about this model is by using the meta-phor of an organisation. If you want to take the performance of an organisation to the next level you could change the administrative staff. Things could be better organised but the overall performance is unlikely to improve. If you bring in a new CEO with a dynamic vision, that energy is likely to filter down through all the levels of the organisation.

So, if you want to make effective, long-lasting change, you need to make changes at the highest levels of your brain function.

Robert Dilts took this concept and developed the model of Neurological Levels. He proposed six levels :

Purpose/Spiritual	For whom? For what?
Identity	Who?
Values & Beliefs	Why?
Capabilities and Resources	How?
Behaviour	What?
Environment	Where?

Starting at the highest level, the Purpose or Spiritual level is about our sense of being part of something bigger than ourselves. This thinking takes place at the level of collective consciousness. I ask my clients "If you had a purpose in life, a reason to be on this earth, what would it be?" The answers range from "to be a good mother/father" to "to help others" to "to enjoy myself". A few clients have no answer. There is plenty of evidence to show that people who have a sense of purpose live longer and happier lives.

The level of identity is about who we think we are. It brings together our beliefs, capabilities, and behaviour. It can be associated with the nervous system as a whole and probably involves deep brain structures. Change or transformation of identity can have an almost instantaneous effect on the physiology.

Values and beliefs are fundamental judgements and evaluations about ourselves, others, and the world around us. Our values motivate us to do something or keep doing something. Beliefs organise our model of the world. They can produce changes in the fundamental physiological functions. This is the basis for how polygraphs or lie-detectors work.

Capabilities and resources are the mental strategies and internal maps people develop to guide their behaviours. This is a level of experience. You can remember things from the past and imagine things in the future. It involves mastery over behaviour. Neurologically it is a function of the cortex of the brain.

Behaviour relates to the physical actions and reactions through which we interact with the people and environment around us. It is a result of activity in our motor systems. The psychomotor system coordinates our physical actions and conscious movements.

At the lowest level, our environment is made up of factors such as external surroundings, weather conditions, noise, temperature etc. We receive environmental information through our senses. The peripheral nervous system is responsible for producing sensations and reflex reactions.

If you want to make effective changes in your life, it makes sense to involve all of your NLLs. If you only make changes at the lower level it is unlikely to be successful or long-lasting. For example, think about people who want to lose weight and join one of the popular slimming programmes. They are encouraged to make changes to their behaviour, what they eat and how they exercise, but they don't examine their beliefs and values. What generally happens is that they lose weight and then go back to their old ways of eating and behaving and what happens next? They put the weight back on and a bit more.

In my experience people who have well-aligned neurological levels are emotionally and mentally strong. Their values and beliefs support their identity. Their behaviour helps them to develop the capabilities and resources they need to pursue their purpose. When you meet them you feel their purpose shining through. They are totally congruent.

The chart below shows an example of two women, one congruent with her NLLs, and who is incongruent with her NLLs.

	Incongruent	Congruent
Purpose	To make a difference in women's lives	To make a difference in women's lives
Identity	A person enjoying the good life	A healthy, balanced, inspiring woman
Values and beliefs	Having a good time is the most important thing Making money I don't need to work at it If it doesn't work, I can give up and do something else.	My health is important Giving something back to society I want to be a good role model Women are important to the welfare of society I want to live into a healthy old age Hard work yields results
Resources & Capabilities	Learning about business skills	Learning about business skills Researching women's health issues
Behaviour	Eating and drinking what I want Networking Selling Self-promotion Out drinking with friends	Living a healthy lifestyle Networking Collaborating Public speaking Developing skills Volunteering
Environment	Office Sofa in front of the TV	Office Workshops and seminars Gym

In the example above, both women want to help other women and some elements of their NLLs are the same. But the differences mean that their outcomes will be different.

As you move up the neurological levels you mobilize a deeper commitment of the nervous system. Spend time clarifying your purpose and your identity and you are more likely to achieve your goals.

You can also use NLLs to supercharge the changes you want to make in your life.

Exercise

Visualising You with Your Goal Achieved

Take a moment to think about the change you want to make or the goal you want to achieve.

Now imagine that you have achieved your goal. Get a clear sense of what that would be like. Ask yourself the following questions. What is different when you have achieved your goal?

- **Environment** What do you see, hear, and feel? What is around you, including the people?

- **Behaviour** What are you doing differently? What actions are you taking?

- **Resources** What skills or abilities have you developed to make this possible? Are they ones you currently have or are they new?

- **Beliefs** What does the you achieving your purpose believe about herself, that by believing it has helped her achieve her goal?

- **Values** What is important to that future you that motivated you to keep moving towards your goal?

- **Identity** Who are you with your goal achieved? "I am . . ."

- **Purpose** How does achieving your goal support your purpose?

Write down your answers as though you have already achieved your goal. Make it a full sensory experience by picturing you with your goal achieved in full technicolour and 3-D. Imagine how it will feel and double those good feelings in your body. Turn up the volume on the positive thoughts. Let your brain know just how important this is.

Summary of NLLs

Our brains function through a hierarchy of neurological levels.

To make long-lasting, effective change we need to engage all the levels of our brains.

Making changes at the higher functional levels is likely to cause changes at the lower levels.

Making changes only at the lower functional levels is unlikely to have any effect on the higher levels.

Alignment of the neurological levels brings congruency.

For Bonus Gifts go to:
www.hotwomencoolsolutions.com

UNDERSTANDING YOUR PURPOSE

Purpose: *"Our sense of being part of something beyond ourselves. Related to our sense of mission in life. For whom and for what." Dilts, R.*

"I've come to believe that each of us has a personal calling that's as unique as a fingerprint—and that the best way to succeed is to discover what you love and then find a way to offer it to others in the form of service, working hard, and also allowing the energy of the universe to lead you." Oprah Winfrey

"Life-fulfilling work is never about the money—when you feel true passion for something, you instinctively find ways to nurture it." Ellen Fisher, Fashion Designer

"All through history, there have been movements where business was not just about the accumulation of proceeds but also for the public good." Anita Roddick, founder of The Body Shop.

The final question that I ask all of my clients during our first session is the biggest question, "If you had a purpose, a reason to be on this earth, what would it be?" Some clients look at me blankly. It is something they have never thought about. Others know what I am talking about immediately and they say things such as; "To make a difference", "To help people", "To make a contribution", or "To leave a positive legacy".

The common element in all these statements is that they take the person outside of themselves and connect them with something bigger than they are. Your purpose takes you outside the ego and in contact with the spiritual. I am not using "spiritual" in a narrow sense but in the widest sense. I love this definition of spiritual, "The force that gives life to the body of all living things . . . the fundamental, emotional, and activating principle of a person." You can interpret it as God, the Universe, the Great Spirit, the Source, or whatever for you is the thing that is bigger than you are.

To explain this I use the metaphor of computers. If you are like a personal computer, you have a lot of processing ability stored within you. But, if you connect to the Internet, you have a vastly greater access to information and knowledge. When you connect to your purpose, you become much more powerful.

When you set out your purpose clearly you appeal to people's feelings, their gut reaction. In neurological terms, you are speaking to their limbic system (Sinek, 2009). This is the part of the brain that is responsible for human behaviour and decision making. It often contradicts our rational and analytical understanding of a situation. Express your purpose clearly and not only will you will feel more powerful, people will respond to your new power.

Your sense of purpose may develop with time. Initially I thought my purpose was about learning in order to share knowledge and help people to heal themselves. I now realise that these are my values. (see Chapter 4) I now define my purpose as "To inspire women to lead their best lives after 50."

Some examples of "powerful purpose" statements:

- "Helping people achieve something they did not know was possible." Cinda Turkata, Xindana Technologies

- "Setting myself huge, apparently unachievable challenges and trying to rise above them." Richard Branson, Founder of The Virgin Group

- "I want to put a ding in the universe." Steve Jobs, co-founder of Apple.

- "We believe that we are on the face of the earth to make great products and that's not changing. We are constantly focusing on innovating. We believe in the simple not the complex." Tim Cook, CEO of Apple

- "Inspiration, innovation, integrity." Jo Malone, founder of Jo Malone fragrances

- "Our vision is to be earth's most customer centric company; to build a place where people can come to find and discover anything they might want to buy online." Amazon

- "Creating global solutions to common problems." Steig Westerberg, Founder and CEO Stream Theory

- "Leave it in a better shape than you found it." Samuel Palmisano, CEO of IBM 2001-2012

If you already have a strong sense of purpose, well done! You can move on to the next chapter. If you are not sure or you have never thought about it, read on.

The role of money

You may be thinking that if you are starting up as an entrepreneur then your purpose is to make money. Wrong! Money may come as a result of what you do, it is not the reason you do it. Economist Joseph Alois Schumpeter (1883–1950) suggests that entrepreneurs are not necessarily motivated by profit but regard it as a standard for measuring achievement and success.

Making money may be one of your values and in the short term it may motivate you but in the long term it will not keep you moving forward. That is because money is an extrinsic motivator; it is something outside of you. Money is something that you exchange to meet personal needs. You could describe it as an "energy." Enough is plenty.

Many highly successful business people use their money to set up charitable foundations that enable them to achieve their purpose. Think about Bill Gates, George Lucas, Mark Zuckerberg, Warren Buffet, and Anita Roddick.

There are a number of questions that you can ask yourself that will help you to define your Purpose. Take some time now to do this Exercise.

Exercise

The following questions are prompts for you to think about your purpose. Set aside some time to sit quietly. Consider each question carefully and note down your thoughts and answers.

1. What do I want to create in the world that is beyond me?

2. How do I want to be remembered?

3. What do I want to be remembered for?

4. What would I be proudest to hear people saying about what I am achieving?

5. Who else am I serving?

6. What is my sense of a connection to the wider picture?

7. What would I be proudest to see written on my gravestone?

Now write down your purpose.

"I am passionate about. . . .

The final word goes to Oprah Winfrey, "Your passion should feel like breathing; it's that natural."

Summary

Developing a sense of purpose will give a clear direction to your actions.

Money may be the result of being an entrepreneur but it is not the purpose.

Your sense of purpose connects you with that which is greater than you are.

REVEAL YOUR TRUE IDENTITY

Identity*: "Our sense of who we are. Determines our sense of mission, role, and purpose." Dilts, R.*

"There is a vitality, a life force, a quickening [energy] that is translated through you into action, and because there is only one of you in all time, this expression is unique. If you block it, it will never exist through any other medium and be lost . . . It is your business to keep the channel open." Martha Graham, dance pioneer

"Trust yourself. Create the kind of self that you will be happy to live with all your life. Make the most of yourself by fanning the tiny, inner sparks of possibility into flames of achievement." Golda Meir

"Love yourself first, and everything else falls into line. You really have to love yourself to get anything done in the world." Lucille Ball

When I ask clients to tell me who they are, starting with the words "I am . . .", a frequent answer is "Happy." Happy is not an identity, unless you are one of Snow White's Seven Dwarfs! Happy is an emotion which, like all emotions, is transitory.

Your identity relates to your sense of who you are. It organises your lower level NLLs, your values, beliefs, and capabilities, into a single system. It is the answer to the question "Who?"

What you do for a living does not define who you are as a person. There are many facets to your identity. Think of yourself as a beautiful diamond with lots of shining facets that make up the whole you.

Some words that can be used to describe the identities of successful entrepreneurs: explorer, catalyser, connector, enabler, builder, carrier, and co-creator (Dilts, 2015).

Your past and future identities

You may have many identities in your lifetime such as daughter, student, girlfriend, employee, team member, mother, and friend. Each of these identities may conjure up a different image and feeling for you. Some may feel more positive and stronger than others.

Take a moment now to visualise yourself in a few of these identities. Notice how you picture yourself in these roles. What do you see as you look at yourself? What are you wearing? How are you standing? How does it make you feel? Have you automatically changed your posture? Notice how these identities can bring about immediate changes in your physiology.

Now think about your answer to the question of identity in Chapter 1. Who are you when you have achieved your purpose? Some possible answers:

- A successful entrepreneur

- A generous philanthropist

- A role model for other women

- An active member of the community

- A global influencer
- A catalyst for change

Now visualise yourself as an entrepreneur. Notice how you look, how you stand, and how you feel. Is that image provoking a positive or negative emotion? If it is a negative emotion, ask yourself "what's that about?" Change your physiology, that is sit up straighter, chest up, chin up, eyes gazing out strongly. Has anything changed now in how you respond to that image?

The most powerful state is to be deeply connected with your identity and understand how you respond in the moment. Sometimes we disconnect from our true selves due to trauma or situations that we perceive as threatening to our safety. In these circumstances we can become withdrawn and shut down the channel to our authentic selves. It is not helpful as an entrepreneur to be moving away from what you fear and to be less connected to what you want to do and be.

In a fearful state you can start to believe your limiting beliefs (see Chapter 5) and start telling yourself the stories that mean you cannot achieve your purpose. You might find it harder to deal with difficult feelings and emotions. Your body and posture will reflect your fear.

If you responded negatively to picturing yourself as an entrepreneur, spend some time looking at your values and beliefs in the following chapters. You may need professional help to overcome your limiting beliefs.

What does "success" mean to you?

The idea of "being a success" in your enterprise relates to the level of identity and is strongly related to you satisfying your ego. Society tends to measure success through tangible objects such as wealth and possessions. Success at the inner level is related to the inner experience of gratitude and generosity, the things that money cannot buy. For an illustration of this, read Marci Shimoff's story in Part 2.

Gratitude is about acknowledging and valuing what you have. When you are grateful you are more likely to feel successful.

Generosity is about understanding that you have enough resources and being able to share them with others. If you try to hold onto everything you have you are likely to worry about needing more of it.

Keeping a gratitude journal is a good way to train yourself to notice the many gifts you are given every day. Buy an attractive notebook which you can keep by your bed. At the end of each day, before you go to sleep, write in your journal at least three things that you are grateful for.

Who are you now?

To understand who you are, it is informative to know more about your personality traits. To be confident in pursuing your purpose, you need to understand your strengths and be aware of your development areas. Understanding your personality traits helps you to communicate effectively and to understand others. In the Resources section I have included a link to the Myers Briggs website where you can take a personality trait test.

There are other personality tests that you can take such as Big Five, and Enneagram. There are website links in Resources. These types of tests can provoke you into thinking more about how you see yourself and how others might see you. If you use them, notice which parts of the analysis you relate strongly to and which parts you do not recognise.

Use the outcomes of these exercises to build on your strengths, forgive your weaknesses, and take action on the development areas that will support your purpose.

Exercise 1

Using NLLs to determine your Identity (Dilts 2015)

Reflect on and then answer the following questions;

1. When and where do you feel most like yourself?

2. What do you do that makes you feel most yourself?

3. What capabilities and skills do you have that most represent you?

4. What do you value? What is most important to you?

5. What do you consider to be your essence?

What did you learn about yourself from this exercise? Were there any common themes running through the different levels?

Exercise 2

Who are you in your story?

Use these questions to increase your awareness of the story you are telling yourself about who you are:

1. When you were growing up, what was your favourite story, film, or game? What was the theme of the story?

2. What is your favourite story, film, or game now? What is the theme of that story?

3. What are the similarities between the stories?

4. What are the similarities between those stories and your own life so far?

5. What have you learned from this about who you are?

Exercise 3

Who are you as an entrepreneur? (Lazarus, 2010)

Use these questions to form a clearer image of you as an entrepreneur:

1. What is your sense of yourself as an entrepreneur?

2. What sort of entrepreneur are you?

3. Could you describe yourself using an analogy, such as "I am like a bear"?

Exercise 4

Getting to know your selves. (McKenna, 2004)

We often have more than one identity. There is the one we pretend to be to mask our fears, the one we are afraid we are, and our authentic self. Use these questions to examine these three selves.

a) Who you pretend to be:

    a. Which aspects of your personality do you hope people notice first?

    b. What is the most important thing that you want everyone to know about you?

    c. If your life was about proving something about you, what would it be?

b) Who you are afraid you are:

    a. Who is your least favourite person and why?

    b. Which of your secrets will only be discovered when you die?

    c. What are your personality traits that you don't want people to know?

c) Who you truly are;

    a. Who are you when nobody is watching?

    b. If you felt totally safe, what would you do differently?

    c. Who would you be if you lived beyond fear?

Summary

Your identity, who you think you are, organises the lower NLLs, particularly your beliefs and capabilities.

Staying connected to your authentic self allows you to pursue your purpose.

Build on your strengths, forgive your weaknesses, and take action on the development areas that are relevant to your purpose.

Check-in point

How does your identity support your Purpose?

For Bonus Gifts go to:
www.hotwomencoolsolutions.com

CHAPTER 4

UNDERSTAND WHAT MOTIVATES YOU

Values: "At the core of motivation and culture. Answers the question 'Why?' " Dilts, R

"I believe in business where you engage in creative thinking, and where you form some of your deepest relationships. If it isn't about the production of the human spirit, we are in big trouble." Anita Roddick

"We learned about honesty and integrity—that the truth matters . . . that you don't take shortcuts or play by your own set of rules . . . and success doesn't count unless you earn it fair and square." Michelle Obama

"The important thing to note is that it is not important whether Malala was shot or not—Malala is not asking for personal favours or support. She is asking for support with girls' education and women's rights. So don't support Malala, support her campaign for girls' education and women's rights." Malala Yousafzai

"Love is your job description—no matter what you do for a living. If you ever feel unsure of what you're supposed to do in a situation,

here's a good rule of thumb: always do what leads to greater love."
Marci Shimoff, Best-Selling Author of Happy for No Reason

Back in 1999 I started to read The *7 Habits of Highly Successful People* by Stephen R Covey. I was zipping through it until I got to the chapter about values. Covey says that values are "internal and subjective and represent that which we feel strongest about in guiding our behaviour." There is a difference between principles and values. Covey states that "Principles are natural laws that are external to us and that ultimately control the consequences of our actions."

No one had ever asked me what my values were. I stalled on that chapter for about a year.

Values and beliefs act as powerful unseen filters in our brains that filter and make sense of our experience. We are not generally aware of them operating in the unconscious parts of our brain.

Our values are the things that motivate and help us to prioritise our actions and decisions. We add a value to things that we do and people that we know and then, when we have to decide whether to take action or favour one person over another, our unconscious consults the ranking and the decision is made. We have very little knowledge how this decision is being made and we rationalise it after the event.

Have you ever made an arrangement to go somewhere for a work-related event and then another option was presented to you and you chose the new event? Your internal values weighed up the options and the choice was made. If you enjoy the new event, you will add even more value to it and would be more likely to choose it again in the future. If it was a bad experience, you will lower its value.

Your values come from your life experiences. They are influenced by various factors including your upbringing, family, education, friends, community, religion, and the media. Your values can change over time. When you are young and single you have a very different set of priorities than when you have children. They are also context dependent, that is, you may have different values relating to your career, relationships, and buying choices.

Your values, when aligned with your purpose and identity, will help you to stay on course and to hold yourself accountable for the things that you are doing. Simon Sinek (2009) suggests that to be truly effective, our values should be written out as verbs, for example not "integrity" but "always doing the right thing." In that way our values become a discipline.

Becoming aware of your values helps you to make more conscious decisions and to be aware of conflicting values. This is very important to new entrepreneurs. Let me explain. Let's say that you think your financial security is very important but you are unaware that your personal development is also a very strong motivator. You may find yourself sabotaging your business because you are spending so much time trying to make money that you have no time to take any courses.

If you are developing your business with partners, it is equally important to understand their values. You may all have agreed that the most important thing is that the business makes money but if you place a high value around giving back to society this may give rise to internal conflict. The business may be making money but, if the partnership has not made any provision for charitable donations, you might feel dissatisfied.

And that is an important point. When our personal values are not met we feel uncomfortable and dissatisfied. Our decision making mechanism is not being allowed to function correctly and our ego becomes depleted with every contradictory decision we make.

Values, brand, and authenticity

If you are setting out as solopreneur you may not think you have brand, but you do. You may not even think that having a brand is important, but it is. Your brand lives in other people's heads; it is what they say about you. If they say that you are kind and considerate and hard-working, that is part of your personal brand. If they say that you are well-meaning but always late and disorganised, that is part of your brand.

I have a friend who is a therapist. Whenever her clients talk about her they always say things like, "I love going to see her. She always makes me smile. We have great chats. It is so relaxing." They like her and trust her. A good brand for a therapist.

When you are clear about your values and you live up to them, your personal brand strengthens. If you set out your values but they do not align with your actions, you will not be perceived to be authentic and your brand will not be authentic. Authenticity means that you actually believe in everything that you say and do.

Look again at the quotes at the beginning of this chapter and notice the values that are being setting out. Malala Yousafzai has a value around girls' education. If she dropped out of school, how much would you want to support her cause? If Michelle Obama says that "the truth matters" and then she is caught in a significant untruth, what would it do to her personal brand and any cause she supports? Think about what happened to "family man" Tiger Woods after his private behaviour came to light.

My purpose is "To inspire women to live their best lives, regardless of age." My top values are learning, sharing, healing, and serving. That is why I am writing these words on a Sunday afternoon when I could be sitting in front of the television with a glass of wine! I love what I do and I want to share it. However, I am only human so please forgive me if sometimes I do not get it right.

If you believe strongly in your purpose and you want other people to support you, make sure that your values are aligned with what you want to achieve. That is the way to authenticity.

Exercise

Values elicitation

There is a simple exercise that you can do to help you understand and rank your values. You can do it alone or with a partner, preferably someone to facilitate you and keep you "honest."

The first stage is to ask yourself, or have someone ask you, "What is important about [your new enterprise]?" Make a note of your answers down the left hand side of the table below. Keep asking the question until you have a list of about ten values. Do not worry about the ranking at this stage.

Review the list. Does it look about right?

Next, take the first value and compare it to all the others in the list one by one. Ask yourself "which is more important to me right now?" If you could have one of these values and not the other, which would you choose? Put a tick next to the value which is most important.

When you have worked down the list, comparing the first value to all the other values, do the same with the second value on the list. Work down the list doing this for all the values. Make sure you always compare a value to the values below it to avoid double counting

When you have finished comparing all of the values, see which of your values have the highest number of ticks. These are your most important values.

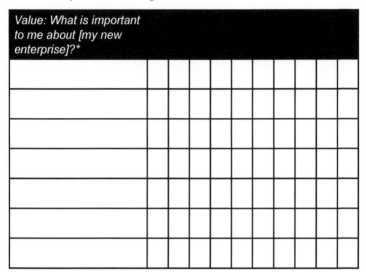

Value: What is important to me about [my new enterprise]?*										

*Values associated with pursuing your purpose could include: personal development, giving back to society, learning, sharing knowledge, financial security, supporting others, spreading my message, leading a balanced life, using my skills, being creative, and leading a fulfilled life.

You can take this exercise a stage further to clarify your values by asking yourself or having someone ask you what you specifically mean by each value. For example, if you have a value around "helping more people" it would be useful to understand more about what you mean by "helping" and "which" people.

Now consider how these values will be satisfied in your new enterprise. What more could you do to satisfy your values? Remember, this is what will keep you motivated during difficult times.

If you have a business partner, or are thinking of going into partnership, ask your partner to do the same exercise and then compare your top values. If they are the same, ask each other what those values mean to you in your business relationship. How are they present in your business? Could you do something to give them higher priorities?

If your values are significantly different, what can you both do to satisfy the other person's needs? What can they do to satisfy your values? If your values are in conflict, how can you resolve them? For example, if you have a value around "giving back to the community" and your partner has a value around "making a good return to investors," how can you do that in a way that honours both of your values?

A partner who does not share your values can seriously affect your personal brand, the brand of your enterprise, and the day-to-day operation of the business.

Summary

Values are "what is important to you"—"what you want or seek."

Values inform your decision making process.

Along with beliefs, values filter the information you receive and make sense of your experience.

When your actions are congruent with your values, you will be perceived as authentic.

If you are going to work with partners, you will be most effective if you share common values.

Check-in point

How do your values align with and support your Purpose and your Identity?

THE POWER OF BELIEFS

Beliefs: "Generalisations about the world and our opinions about it. They form the rules about what we can and cannot do." Lazarus (2010)

"Always aim high, work hard, and care deeply about what you believe in. And, when you stumble, keep faith. And, when you're knocked down, get right back up and never listen to anyone who says you can't or shouldn't go on." Hillary Clinton, US Presidential Candidate

"Aerodynamically the bumblebee shouldn't be able to fly, but the bumblebee doesn't know that so it goes on flying anyway." Mary Kay Ash, Founder of Mary Kay Cosmetics

"If you think you are too small to have an impact, try going to bed with a mosquito." Anita Roddick, founder of The Body Shop

"Every time you state what you want or believe, you're the first to hear it. It's a message to both you and others about what you think is possible. Don't put a ceiling on yourself." Oprah Winfrey, O Magazine, 2003

Beliefs provide support for or inhibit our capabilities and behaviours. They form in the limbic system of the brain and give rise to physiological responses such as heart pounding, skin tingling, and stomach tightening. Your experience of life is strongly influenced by your beliefs.

Beliefs come from many different sources, for example: parents, family, teachers, peers, society, books, and other media. The beliefs you form in early life are the strongest. This may be because beliefs are also stronger when they come from someone with high status. So, beliefs that you acquire from your parents and school teachers when you are young are likely to be very powerful and harder to challenge and change.

Beliefs are powerful because we treat them as factual even though they rarely are. They feel true because you look for evidence to support the things that you believe. We generally only adopt an opposite belief when there is strong evidence to support the new view.

A simple example. When you were young, your mum and dad probably told you all about Father Christmas. You saw pictures of him, you sent him letters, and maybe you met him and sat on his lap. You received most of the gifts you had asked him for. You totally believed in him.

Then, one day, someone you trusted, a friend or sibling, started to sow the seeds of doubts and you started to question the evidence. How could he visit every home in the world in one night? How did he deliver presents to houses without chimneys? How come he wore your dad's shoes? You now wonder how you could ever have believed in him.

You will probably have experienced this belief flip multiple times in your life. There was that young man that you believed was the love of your life or the job you thought was perfect. Maybe you have changed political allegiance or stopped believing in the religion you were raised in. In all of these cases the evidence to support the original belief is still there but the evidence for the new belief has become stronger and outweighed it.

The fact that beliefs can change is a good thing, as you will soon discover.

Types of beliefs

There are two types of beliefs. Some beliefs are enabling, that is they can help you to achieve the results you desire. If you believe that this is an exciting and liberating stage in your life, you will have a positive experience. You will take action to achieve your purpose.

Other beliefs are limiting and they get in the way of the action you need to take. If you believe that your life will be all downhill after your 50th birthday, then you will notice all the things that prove that belief. You will be less likely to try to achieve your dreams.

Beliefs are powerful blocks to action. Over 35% of people say the fear of failure stops them exploiting the business opportunities they see.

The chart below shows some examples of both types of beliefs.

Enabling Belief	Limiting Belief
"I'll give it a try, what's the worst that can happen?"	"I'll look stupid if I fail."
"Mistakes are just feedback."	"Mistakes mean failure."
"I can ask if I need help."	"Asking for help is a sign of weakness."
"I can learn how to do that."	"I'll never be any good at that."
"With work I can achieve my goals."	"Nothing I do makes a difference."
"It's never too late to do something you feel strongly about."	"I'm too old to do something new."

Exercise 1

Change your beliefs

Step 1: Make a list of the limiting beliefs that may stop you from pursuing your purpose. Decide which is your most powerful limiting belief. Spend a week acting as if that belief is not true. Notice the evidence that it is not true.

Step 2: Think about an enabling belief that would support you in pursuing your purpose. Spend a week acting as if the enabling belief were true. Notice the evidence that the new belief is true.

Exercise 2

Another technique is to identify the limiting beliefs and create positive statements to replace them.

Step 1: Start by identifying your beliefs, both limiting and empowering. Consider what each belief implies. Be specific.

My Beliefs I am smart.	My pay-offs or consequences I feel confident that I can succeed.

Step 2: Take your limiting beliefs and decide which ones you want to get rid of.

a) Write out your limiting beliefs on the left side of a sheet of paper. Keep it simple such as "I am too old." "I don't have enough time."

b) Now write the opposite statement on the right side of the page. Write it larger and bolder.

c) Repeat your positive statements out loud 10 times every day, saying it louder each time.

d) Refer to your list daily for 21 days.

Limiting Belief	Positive statement

Summary

Our beliefs come from a variety of sources such as parents, teachers, society, religion, and media.

Beliefs that form when we are young or come from someone of high status are more powerful.

Beliefs can be changed if you look for and find evidence to support the new belief

Beliefs come in two types, limiting beliefs and enabling beliefs.

Check-in point

How do your beliefs support your identity and purpose?

Do you have limiting beliefs that you need to challenge?

For Bonus Gifts go to
www.hotwomencoolsolutions.com

EXPLORE YOUR CAPABILITIES

Capabilities: "The mental strategies and maps we develop to guide our behaviour. Capability involves mastery over a class of behaviour." Dilts, R.

"We need to accept that we won't always make the right decisions, that we'll screw up royally sometimes—understanding that failure is not the opposite of success, it's part of success." Ariana Huffington, Editor-in-Chief of Huffington Post

"Don't be intimidated by what you don't know. That can be your greatest strength and ensure that you do things differently from everyone else." Sara Blakely, founder of Spanx

There are three types of capabilities that you need to be an entrepreneur; managerial, technical, and entrepreneurial.

If you are a solopreneur and performing all three roles, be aware of how much time you are spending in each area. If you are spending most of your time doing technical and managerial work, you are working in your business. If you spend your time doing entrepreneurial work, you are working on your business. There needs to be a balance.

Managerial skills

Let's start by looking at the managerial skills you need to run any business. The table below shows some common managerial skills.

Accounting	Administration	Book keeping
Business Planning	Creativity	Decision making
Design	Finance	Human Resources
IT Skills	Management	Marketing
Negotiation	Networking	Presentations
Project Management	Research	Sales
Social Media	Time management	Writing copy

This is not an exhaustive list. Depending on the nature of your purpose, you may not need all of these skills or you may need additional skills such as leadership, data management, or legal knowledge.

What is important about this list is to understand that you may not have all the capabilities you need—yet, and that is okay. You cannot do everything yourself. Being an entrepreneur is not a solitary pursuit. It is about understanding your strengths so that you can make the most of them. It is also about understanding the things you are not so good at or don't enjoy doing and then finding support to fill those gaps.

You will be most effective when you are using your strongest capabilities, the things you enjoy doing the most. I love being creative. When I get frustrated in my business, I look for the opportunity to create something in that situation.

I also love making presentations and I am most energised and resourceful when I am presenting ideas to others. If I am unable to do something or I come up against an obstacle, I imagine presenting the problem to a group and often the solution comes to mind.

Exercise 1

Audit your managerial skills

i. Using the table above as a guide, make a list of the capabilities and skills you already have.

ii. Highlight or underline your areas of excellence, the things you are best at or most enjoy.

iii. Make a list of the skills you think you need in your business.

iv. Which of those skills do you want to acquire personally? How will you acquire them? For example by reading, attending courses, skills swap, on-line webinars, etc

v. How can you acquire the remaining skills, such as hiring new staff, outsourcing, joint venture etc?

Technical skills

Depending on the nature of your business or your entrepreneurial idea, you may need specific technical skills. For example, as a Cognitive Hypnotherapist, I have a qualification that is recognised by a national regulating organisation. That not only means that I can work effectively with my clients but it also gives my clients confidence in my abilities and enables me to obtain professional insurance.

You may have a self-taught skill that you are developing into a business. You need to consider how you will convince customers that you have the skills they are looking for. If you are looking for financial support for your new enterprise, you may be required to demonstrate your technical skills to financiers.

Many women who have a technical skill that they enjoy practising can find themselves spending too much time on one-to-one work and neglecting the pursuit of their purpose. I know lots of brilliant therapists who love the work they do with clients. That is great but they have no time to move their business from one-to-one to one-to-many. Pursuing a purpose is definitely one-to-many.

Exercise 2

Audit your technical skills

What technical skills do you need to achieve your purpose?

How will you acquire those skills?

Is there a regulating body for those skills that you will need to satisfy?

Entrepreneurial skills

Managers and technicians are rooted in the present. Entrepreneurs are looking to the future. Entrepreneurs can drive managers crazy when they keep disrupting processes with their new thoughts and ideas.

Being an entrepreneur is not a "job". Richard Branson has never worked in any of his companies, except at the beginning when he was selling vinyl records out of cardboard boxes in Oxford Street! An entrepreneur is "Someone who exercises initiative by organising a venture to take benefit of an opportunity and, as the decision maker, decides what, how, and how much of a good or service will be produced." Or ". . . supplies risk capital as a risk taker, and monitors and controls the business activities . . . usually a sole proprietor, a partner, or the one who owns the majority of shares in an incorporated venture." (BusinessDictionary.com)

Entrepreneurs look for the gap between what customers want and need, and what is currently available. They take a risk to produce goods or services to fill that gap. Entrepreneurs serve as the spark plug in the economy's engine, stimulating activity.

The capabilities required to be an entrepreneur include: creativity, forward thinking, energetic, risk-taking, resilience, determination, optimism, flexibility, rapid decision making, goal oriented, and leadership. Entrepreneurs believe in their success. They must be able to sell their ideas to others by convincingly presenting their visions.

If that list seems a bit daunting, remember that aligning your NLLs will help you to discover those capabilities within you. Everything becomes possible when you have a purpose that you feel passionate about, an identity as an entrepreneur, values around creativity and goal achievement, and enabling beliefs in what you can achieve.

Exercise 3

Audit your entrepreneurial skills

Do setbacks motivate you to try harder?

Do you have a clear vision of where the business will take you?

Can you turn your ideas into a business?

Do you know how to evaluate your business?

Your key capabilities and character strengths

You will already have certain skills and capabilities that you excel at. It could be something like networking, problem solving, dealing with finances, negotiating, or big picture thinking. You will be most effective and successful when you are in a role that requires those skills. The challenge is to recognise them and leverage them in your new enterprise.

Your special skill may seem like nothing special to you because it feels so easy to you when you are using it. It is an area where you have mastery. Other people notice it but you may not. When you are using these skills you are more likely to feel the state of "flow" when you are totally immersed in what you are doing and have an energised focus.

Take a moment now to think about your key capabilities. Are you aware what your key capabilities are? What do other people say to you that you do well? What do other people say to you that they wish they could do as well as you? What strengths have been identified in work reviews?

If you have found these questions difficult to answer you could identify some people whom you trust and who know you in a work context. Ask them to give you feedback on your key capabilities. You might be surprised by what they say.

You will also have key character strengths. Character strengths are "the psychological ingredients for displaying human goodness and they serve as pathways for developing a life of greater value . . . character strengths are the positive components—what's best in you" VIA Institute.

The 24 character strengths developed by Christopher Peterson and Martin Seligman, fall under six broad virtues (wisdom, courage, humanity, justice, temperance, and transcendence) and encompass our capacities for helping ourselves and others. Whereas most personality assessments focus on negative and neutral traits, the VIA Character Survey focuses on what is best in you and is at the centre of the science of well-being.

Understanding your character strengths will enable you to live a happier life, build better relationships, improve your health, boost your performance, and accomplish goals. All of this is essential to sustaining your entrepreneurial mojo.

Exercise 4

Discover your character strengths

Take the VIA Survey of Character Strengths and identify your top five signature strengths (see the link in Resources).

How are your top five strengths currently present in your life?

How will your top five strengths support you in achieving your purpose?

Supplement your skills and capabilities.

I have already said that being an entrepreneur requires a multiplicity of capabilities and you can be expected to excel at all of them. Some of the roles you need to take on as an entrepreneur can seem incompatible such as when you want to spend time dealing with clients using your technical skills while your entrepreneurial side wants to be carrying out research.

There are plenty of options for supplementing your skills, for example delegating, outsourcing, and joint ventures.

Delegation. Delegating is the act of assigning another person to do a task on your behalf. It normally refers to a manager transferring a task to an employee or subordinate. If you are setting up a company to pursue your purpose, this will be an option.

Outsourcing. Outsourcing involves contracting out part of your business process to another party. Using a virtual personal assistant is an effective way of dealing with basic administrative work, telephone answering, and diary management.

You can also outsource technical tasks such as website development and maintenance, marketing, and sales. I have outsourced the design of book covers and the editing and formatting of books.

Outsourcing does not need to be expensive. There are many websites that bring together business owners with freelancers based in countries all around the world. See Resources for more details.

Choose the people or companies that you outsource to carefully. You want to be sure that they will deliver the quality you require on time. You also need to protect any sensitive information about your business or your clients. Ask business friends for recommendations.

Joint ventures A joint venture is a "business agreement in which the parties agree to develop, for a finite time, a new entity and new assets by contributing equity. They exercise control over the enterprise and consequently share revenues, expenses, and assets" (Wikipedia).

I have been involved in several joint ventures to co-author books, develop online courses, and run a weekend retreat. The venture can be for one specific project only or a continuing business relationship.

Whenever you are employing staff, outsourcing, or getting involved in joint ventures, refer back to the Chapter 4 on values.

Summary

There are three sets of skills that you require in order to be a successful entrepreneur: managerial, technical, and entrepreneurial.

To be effective and successful, concentrate on using the skills you excel at and enjoy.

Find ways to acquire the other skills by delegating, outsourcing, and joint ventures.

Check-in point:

How will your capabilities support you in achieving your purpose?

How will your key character strengths be present in your new enterprise?

For Bonus Gifts go to
www.hotwomencoolsolutions.com

CHAPTER 7

TAKE ACTION

Behaviour: *"The physical actions and reactions through which we interact with the people and environment around us."* Dilts, R.

"Vision without action is just a dream, action without vision just passes the time, and vision with action can change the world". Nelson Mandela

"I long to accomplish a great and noble task, but it is my chief duty to accomplish humble tasks as though they were great and noble. The world is moved along, not only by the mighty shoves of its heroes, but also by the aggregate of the tiny pushes of each honest worker." Helen Keller, US Blind and Deaf Educator

"I didn't get there by wishing for it or hoping for it, but by working for it." Estee Lauder

"I wake up every morning thinking . . . this is my last day, and I jam everything into it. There's no time for mediocrity. This is no damned dress rehearsal". Anita Roddick, founder of The Body Shop

Many of our behaviours come from our mental maps and internal processes. Neurologically, our external behaviour is a result of activity in our motor system. Behaviours without any inner map, plan, or strategy to guide them are like knee jerk reactions, habits, or rituals.

How many self-help books have you read that started with the importance of visualising where you want to be? You may have thought, "If this is all I have to do to be successful, this will be a piece of cake!" And then further on in the book you realised that you actually had to do something about your dream and you started to lose interest. Recognise that?

If you have read this book from the beginning you should now have that strong image of your purpose supported by your identity, values, beliefs, and capabilities. It is time to plan what you are going to do about it.

When you read the stories of the entrepreneurial women in the second half of this book, you will see just how much action these women took. They carried out research, they acquired new skills, they connected with people, they set up companies, and they created new products and services. What they did, the actions they took, was totally aligned with their purpose.

This is not just about being busy and working hard. If it was, everyone who worked hard would be successful, and they're not. This is about identifying the actions and behaviours that will lead you towards fulfilling your purpose and focussing on doing them.

This chapter is not a complete "how to" guide to setting up in business. It is some suggestions and signposts towards planning your next actions.

What's the problem?

As an entrepreneur, your role is to identify a problem that a large number of people have and developing a product or service that solves it. The bigger the problem you solve, the bigger the reward you will receive.

Stop for a moment now and think about your purpose. What is the big problem that you will solve by pursuing your purpose? You will probably need to do some research into both the problem and the solutions that are already available. Who is your competition? Who is your ideal client?

Developing the profile of your ideal client will involve both demographics (statistical information such as age, location, gender, ethnicity, and occupation), and psychographics (personal behaviour, values, lifestyle, and buying style). You might even want to give him or her a name to make them more real.

When I decided to create a niche around menopause it aligned with my purpose of inspiring women to live their best lives after 50. I did some research into what was generally available to help women experiencing menopause symptoms. The loudest voices on that subject were manufacturers of hormone replacement products.

Then I researched mind/body approaches to menopause and there was a distinct lack of advice from that perspective. There are plenty of hypnotherapy and NLP books on other specialist issues such as slimming, smoking, confidence, sleep, and having a better life. Most of the Best Sellers are written by men and they are unlikely to write a plausible menopause book!

It is a big problem to solve because all women go through menopause whether due to passage of time or to medical treatments or procedures. Of course, not all women experience significant symptoms and, of those who do, some will opt for hormone therapy. That leaves a significant number of women looking for treatment options.

So my ideal clients are not "all women over 40". My ideal clients are women aged between 45 and 65 who are proactive about their health. They are open to complementary approaches and willing to make lifestyle changes in order to have a long and healthy life. They don't expect "magic bullets." They work and enjoy going to spas and having massages and beauty treatments. Can you picture that woman now?

Create your elevator pitch

Once you are clear on your offering and your ideal client, you can create your Elevator Pitch. The Elevator Pitch is based on the idea that if you found yourself in an elevator with your ideal client and had one minute before it reached its destination, how would you pitch your business to them? It should be interesting, memorable, and succinct.

You can use your Elevator Pitch when you are introduced to someone and they ask you, "So what do you do?" You can use your pitch at networking meetings, at the start of presentations, and in your marketing.

Your Elevator Pitch needs to have three elements. It needs to tell people who you are, why you do what you do (your purpose), what you do and how you do it. If you are making a pitch at a networking event, it also needs to include what sort of clients or business contacts you are looking for.

My elevator pitch goes like this, "Hi, I'm Pat Duckworth, the *Hot Woman with Cool Solutions*. I am passionate about inspiring women to live their best lives after 50. I use mind/body techniques to help women control their menopause symptoms. I see clients one-to-one at my therapy rooms or over Skype".

Notice I'm saying "I'm **the** . . .". If you say "I'm **a** . . ." (such as coach, therapist, photographer or other business title), you will be one of many, a commodity. Using "the" makes you unique in what you do.

Write out your pitch and finesse it. When you are happy with it, try it out on a few trusted business contacts. Listen to their feedback. Ask them what they remember from your pitch. Once you feel confident about it, keep rehearsing saying it. It will stop you from wasting time saying "um" and "er" when you are introduced to an influential business contact.

For more guidance on how to craft a memorable Elevator Pitch see Resources.

Plan your work and work your plan

It is time to create a business plan. If you are going to seek financial support or investment for your business you will need a business plan. There are plenty of examples of layouts for business plans on the Internet (see links in Resources).

Business plans generally contain the following elements:

- An executive summary—an overview of the business you want to start. Include the key points of your plan and the key features of your service or product.

- A short description of the business opportunity—who you are, your product or service, why you are offering it, and to whom. Include the timescale for starting the venture.

- Your marketing and sales strategy—why you think people will buy what you want to sell and how you plan to sell to them.

- Your credentials, qualifications, and, if appropriate, the people you plan to recruit to work with you.

- Your operations—your premises, production facilities, your management information systems and IT.

- Financial forecasts—this section translates everything you have said in the previous sections into numbers.

Writing your business plan can help you to spot potential pitfalls in your venture. It will help you to structure the financial side of your business efficiently and to focus on your development efforts. Importantly, it will help you to measure your progress and to celebrate your success.

You are writing your business plan at a certain moment in time. As you know, circumstances change, for example your personal circumstances, market circumstances, and economic circumstances. Think of your business plan as a living document. It is something you should come back to regularly to review your progress and to update the details as your business evolves.

Manage your time

Once you have your high level business plan you can start to organize your targets into daily, weekly, and monthly actions. Your goals require timelines and deadlines to keep you on track.

When I am starting a new project, I like to create a Gantt chart to break the big actions down into smaller, more manageable actions. A Gantt chart is a graphical representation of tasks plotted against the progression of time. You can create one in Excel or use one of the specifically designed applications (see Resources).

A Gantt chart is an example of a time management technique. As an entrepreneur you are going to need good time management practices to balance your work roles. Creating a daily "To Do" list last thing at night for the following day will prepare you for your working day. Our brains love To Do lists. They give us a blast of the hormone dopamine every time we tick something off of the list or reach a target.

To make your To Do list even more effective, prioritise the tasks on it. Review the list at lunchtime every day. You may need to add some more tasks to it because of things that have occurred during the morning. Re-prioritise your list for the afternoon.

At the end of the day review your list again and notice any tasks that you didn't manage to complete. Sometimes the tasks that are left at the end of the day have some element of fear attached to them. Be aware of your motives in not doing the task. What can you do about it?

If you are a new entrepreneur, you need to build your confidence in yourself in this new role. You will do this if you set yourself achievable daily and weekly targets and then deliver them. So make sure that your To Do list is achievable. Break the tasks down into smaller chunks if that makes them more doable.

There are lots more time management techniques that you can use. See the Resources section for links.

Showing up

People will judge your business by how you show up in the world. That is not just how you look, talk, and behave face-to-face but also how you represent yourself on the phone, Skype, your website, and on social media.

If you want to be inspirational, you have to live an inspirational life. You have to model for your ideal clients the benefits of the product or service you are offering. When you are aligned with purpose, identity, values, and beliefs, it should not be difficult to be congruent in your behaviour.

My purpose is about inspiring women to live their best lives after 50, so guess what I am doing? I generally look after myself, eat healthily, exercise regularly, and have fun. I live by the advice that I give others. I love what I do and I am enthusiastic about it, and that is what clients see when they meet me or they interact with me on social media.

That does not mean that I always look perfect and live like a nun. I am only human and I expect my clients to be human too. People respond to you when they recognise your humanity and vulnerability.

Think about what your ideal clients would expect to see from you based on the messages that you are giving them. What would they expect you to look like? Even think about what they would expect you to wear. All of this will depend upon the nature of your purpose and business and will be personal to you. But you can get clues from observing people who are successful in your field of expertise. What can you learn from them and how they behave?

Celebrate!

Remember to celebrate your achievements, the small ones as well as the big ones. As an entrepreneur you will often be working by yourself on a vision that only you can see. Keep yourself motivated by celebrating by yourself and with others. If you publish a book have a launch party. If you complete a big piece of work, go and have afternoon tea with a friend.

Exercise

Plan your next steps

What actions are you already taking towards achieving your purpose?

What behaviours do you use in other situations which may be useful here?

What behaviours are not useful in this context? What can you stop doing?

What can you learn from your competitors' behaviour?

What is the first action are you going to take today?

What action are you going to take tomorrow?

What action are you going to take next week?

What action are you going to take next month?

Summary

Research your entrepreneurial idea.

Understand the demographics and psychographics of your ideal client.

Develop a compelling Elevator Pitch.

Create a business plan that is a living document. Be prepared to change it when circumstances change.

Manage your time and balance your business roles.

Show up authentically in your business.

Check-in point

How will your actions help you to achieve your purpose?

CHAPTER 8

CREATING A SUPPORTIVE ENVIRONMENT

"Your environment is made up of everything that you can perceive through your senses. It includes factors such as your location, your office, and the people around you. Your environment is responsible for producing sensations and reflex reactions." Dilts, R.

"It is a critical job of any entrepreneur to maximize creativity, and to build the kind of atmosphere around you that encourages people to have ideas. That means open structures, so that accepted thinking can be challenged." Anita Roddick, Founder of The Body Shop

"Next time, ask, 'What's the worst that will happen?' Then push yourself a little further than you dare. Once you start to speak, people will yell at you. They will interrupt you, put you down, and suggest it's personal. And the world won't end . . . And the speaking will get easier and easier. And you will find you have fallen in love with your own vision, which you may never have realized you had. And you will lose some friends and lovers, and realize you don't miss them. And new ones will find you and cherish you . . . And at last you'll know with surpassing certainty that only one thing is more frightening than speaking your truth. And that is not speaking." Audre Lorde

"Close friends and relatives, while not meaning to do so, often hand-icap one through 'opinions' and sometimes through ridicule, which is meant to be humorous. Thousands of men and women carry inferi-ority complexes with them all through life, because some well-mean-ing, but ignorant person destroyed their confidence through 'opinions or ridicule.' " Napoleon Hill, <u>Think and Grow Rich</u>

"Who you spend time with is who you become." Nido Qubein, *Businessman, Coach, Philanthropist, and Inspirational Speaker.*

In this chapter I am not going to talk about your prem-ises or location. This is all about the people you surround yourself with who will have an enormous impact on you, positive or negative.

Whatever age you are when you are setting up in business, you need to surround yourself with people who will sup-port and encourage you. These are the sort of people who notice your many small triumphs and encourage you to learn from the things that do not go to plan. They inspire you through their actions and learning. They say things like: "What is the next thing you can do towards your goal?", "You can learn how to do that." and "I know someone who can help you with that."

These people may be business contacts, coaches, friends, or family members. What matters most is their attitude. Search them out.

Remember; emotions are contagious.

If you spend time with positive people you are more likely to be positive. If you spend time with people who are neg-ative, you are more likely to become negative. That is why it is important to avoid or limit your exposure to people who say things like: "That will never work", "You can't do that",

"You will never succeed at . . ." or "Who do you think you are? Richard Branson!"

If you have to spend time with people who have negative attitudes, develop an invisible shield that has the power to repel unhelpful energy and remarks. Visualise wrapping it around yourself whenever one of these people approaches you. See the negative stuff bouncing off your shield with a reassuring "Ping"! Send the energy back with love. You can stand inside your shield, safe and smiling.

Do not ask your family and for business advice unless that is their profession. They love you and their advice will be based in their desire to keep you safe and away from pain. That is not a helpful perspective for an entrepreneur.

Building a network

If you are a new entrepreneur it is essential to set up a network of business contacts. The benefits of networking include:

- Connecting with other business owners

- Developing mutually beneficial relationships

- Marketing your product or service

- Building a group of people you trust and respect

- Exchanging information, advice, and referrals

If you are a solopreneur, attending a regular network group can help you to feel less alone. Attending networking groups can also be a safe way of practising and finessing your Elevator Pitch.

You could network for every hour of every day. You could start with a breakfast meeting, and then move on to a mid-morning coffee group before you go to a lunch group, and so on, ending with an evening gathering. You need to decide what you want to achieve from networking. You may want to achieve a certain number of referrals or build your business's image or brand.

Most networking groups allow you to attend two or three meetings before you have to join. Try a few and find what works best for you and your business before you commit to any annual membership fees. Remember, networking is about building relationships and that takes time. Do not expect overnight results.

I attend a monthly women's network group. At one meeting I was sitting next to a visitor and we were discussing our businesses. I told her what I did and she said, "Wow, I am looking for a Cognitive Hypnotherapist." No one has ever said anything that specific to me but she showed me the search she had used on Google. She immediately booked a session with me and followed up with a second session. She then referred a friend to me who booked in for two sessions. She was so happy with the results that she referred me to a colleague who had four sessions! Eight sessions booked from one conversation.

Mastermind Group

The idea of the mastermind group came from Napoleon Hill's book, *Think and Grow Rich*. He described it as "The coordination of knowledge and effort of two or more people, who work towards a definite purpose in the spirit of harmony."

The benefits of a mastermind group are; mutual support, differing perspectives, resources, and accountability. I would add friendship to that list.

I love my Mastermind Group! In the group is a social media stylist, an artist, a yoga teacher, a therapist, and a coach. We meet every six weeks. We celebrate each other's successes, encourage each other to take the next step, we learn from each other, and we provide a shoulder to cry on when times are tough.

There are no rules about the constitution of mastermind groups but from four to six members seems to be a good number. It does not matter if the members are in the same business as you, what is important is that they share your values.

If you are fortunate, you may be asked to join an existing group. If not, consider starting your own group. Invite people who have a similar drive and commitment. Look for people with diverse skill sets who are prepared to share their knowledge and experience. It is helpful to include people who are good at giving feedback and who are active problem solvers. You all need to commit to regular meetings.

To make those meetings worthwhile give each person the same amount of time to talk about their topic. It is most effective if you have a regular agenda which may include a specific topic for the meeting, such as how to run webinars. You can rotate the role of chair or facilitator so that no one person feels put upon. Celebrate your successes and keep a note of lessons learned from your experiences.

Mentors and Coaches

We all need support and guidance in our businesses. Sometimes we need someone to bounce ideas off of, other times we need someone to give us guidance and suggestions, and other times we need someone who help us to set goals and create a plan.

The terms coaching and mentoring are often used interchangeably but there is a difference between the two roles. Mentors are generally people who have been through the experience that you are going through who are willing to share the lessons they have learned. They can act as a role model for you. The mentoring relationship tends to last longer than a coaching relationship.

Coaches are goal focussed and outcome orientated. They believe that you have all the resources you need to solve your problems even if that resource is about knowing whom you can ask for more help. They are rooted in the present and looking forward to the future. A coach will only dip into your past to identify strategies and behaviour that will help you to achieve your goals. Their role is not to give you advice.

There are many types of coach. You could have a business coach, or a transactional coach who guides you achieving your current goals, or a transformation coach who helps you to set new, amazing goals to reach the next level of your business.

You may find people who are willing to mentor or coach you for free. If you are able to pay for a mentor or coach, do some research into who would fit best with what you want to achieve. Many will offer a free 30 minute consultation or discovery session so that you can ask them questions and they can find out more about your situation. Take advantage of this to find the person and approach that is right for you.

Grow your tribe

So far I have been talking about people who will support you in your business but you also need to think about building your tribe of ideal clients.

Entrepreneur and blogger, Seth Godin, argues that the Internet has ended mass marketing and revived a human social unit from the distant past: tribes. Tribes share ideas and values. They come together with a common purpose and that purpose may change over time.

Your tribe may already exist in other groups, physically or on the Internet. To achieve your purpose, you will want to assemble your tribe and lead them towards your goal. They will follow you, not because they have to but because they believe in you and what you are trying to do.

This is not about mass marketing. Start small with people you respect and trust and ask them to reach out and connect with more like-minded people. Be clear about what you stand for so that your tribe wants to align with you and with similar people. Be authentic and vulnerable so that people connect with your humanity.

Once you have a tribe, inspire and engage with them. Provide a safe environment for them, and encourage them to participate. Always remember that you are the leader. Set the agenda and follow your passion.

For more information about tribes see *Tribes* by Seth Godin.

Exercise

Creating a supportive environment

Whom do you know and respect who will support you in achieving your purpose?

Who in your immediate circle of associates, friends, and family has a negative attitude? How can you limit their impact on you?

What networking groups are in your location or the location of your business?

What do you want to achieve from networking?

Whom would you like to have in your ideal Mastermind Group? What steps can you take to contact them?

Where do your ideal clients gather either in person or online?

What options are there for assembling your tribe—such as regular meetings, Facebook Groups, or Linkedin Groups?

Summary

Surround yourself with people who inspire and support you.

Build a network of business colleagues.

Join or create a Mastermind Group.

Use a mentor or coach to help you to accelerate your business.

Grow your tribe.

Check-in point

How are the people around you supporting you in achieving your purpose?

For Bonus Gifts go to
www.hotwomencoolsolutions.com

THE LAST WORD

Starting out as an entrepreneur can be challenging, even when you have aligned your NLLs. You may be so focussed on achieving your purpose that you do not notice how hard you are working. It is important to take time out to take care of yourself.

There are actions you can take to strengthen your emotional resilience. Some of these I have mentioned in other parts of the book.

1. Acknowledge how you feel, whether positive or negative. If you notice a negative feeling, don't judge it. Go to the mirror and repeat a positive affirmation to yourself. It could be something as simple as "I can do this."

2. Set yourself achievable goals. Don't beat yourself up about the things that don't go right. There is no failure, there is only feedback.

3. Create a supportive network. Seek help from them when you want or need it.

4. Have a laugh every day. Watch something funny on the TV or YouTube. Better still, call a friend who makes you laugh.

5. Commit a random act of kindness every day. It could be as small as a smile to a shop worker or a compliment to a colleague.

6. Connect with nature. Take time each day to notice the things of nature around you. Go for a walk and just look around.

7. Look after your physical health. Eat well and take regular exercise.

8. Practice gratitude. At the end of every day make a note of three gifts you have received. Or write a note of a gift or positive experience on a slip of paper as soon as it happens and put it in a Gratitude Jar that you keep on your desk.

9. Stay in touch with your spirituality. At the start of every day take 10 minutes to meditate, do yoga, or tai chi, or just tune into your breathing. Think about your upcoming day. Notice what thoughts come into your mind.

10. Celebrate your successes. Have fun!

For Bonus Gifts go to
www.hotwomencoolsolutions.com

Part 2

Hot Entrepreneurial Women's Stories

I am grateful to all of the women who have shared their stories with me so that you could learn from them. The stories are all so different and yet have common themes of reaching a change point and deciding to do something new.

As you read them, notice how their Neurological Levels are present in their stories.

Also notice how they faced their challenges and used what they learned to keep taking the next step towards their purpose.

The Happiness High

I was 41 years old, and everything in my life seemed perfect. I had worked hard and achieved all that I thought I needed to be happy.

You see, I was born depressed—I came out of the womb with existential angst. Though I had a wonderful family and great life circumstances during my childhood and teen years, I always felt that there was a dark cloud around me.

So, when I was in my early twenties, I decided to set five goals for myself that I thought would bring me a happy life. My five goals were to have a successful career, a loving husband, a comfortable home, a great body, and fabulous friends. After years of study, hard work, and a few "lucky breaks," I finally had them all. (Okay, so my body didn't quite look like Halle Berry's—but four out of five isn't bad!) You think I'd have been on top of the world.

But surprisingly I wasn't.

One day in 1998 I had a big wake-up call. At the time, three of my Chicken Soup for the Woman's Soul books were in the top five on the New York Times Best Seller list the same week. I had just given a speech to 8,000 women and had signed 5,432 books. My client had even hired a massage therapist to rub my hand every hour as I autographed copy after copy after copy. I felt like an author rock star.

But after autographing that last book, I went up to my hotel room, looked out at the panoramic view of Lake Michigan, and then fell onto my bed and burst into tears. There I was at the height of my success, and I had to admit the awful truth to myself: I still wasn't happy. I felt an emptiness inside that my outer attainments couldn't fill. I was also afraid that if I lost any of those "things," I might be miserable.

I realized I had a big problem. I couldn't continue to acquire or accomplish any more, thinking that would make me happy. At each step of the way, I was excited about the successes I'd achieved, but I noticed that the high never lasted. I was happy about the things in my life, but not really happy. Maybe happiness didn't come from the reasons I had imagined. Maybe happiness didn't come from any reason at all.

Despite all those years of striving to be happy, I had no idea what created real and lasting happiness. Could I actually be "happy for no reason"? This became my burning question, and I embarked on a personal quest to find out.

I started by interviewing scores of happiness experts and delving into the scientific research on happiness from the burgeoning field of Positive Psychology. From there, I interviewed hundreds of happy people from all over the world to find out how they were happy for no reason. I found out that the only difference between unconditionally happy people and everyone else is that they have different habits.

I applied what I learned and practiced the habits of happy people—and it worked! I went from a D+ in happiness to an A. Yes, I'm still a work in progress, but my happiness these days is steady and strong.

I became so excited about my newfound happiness and what I'd learned that knew I had to write a book about it; that's how Happy for No Reason was born. The message of being happy for no reason clearly struck a chord, as the book became a New York Times Best Seller and has been published in 31 languages.

From all of my investigations about happiness, one of the most exciting findings is that we each have a "happiness set-point." And in the same way that we turn up the thermostat at home to get warm on a chilly day, we can raise our happiness set-point to become happier. We just need to learn the habits of happy people. Anyone can raise his or her happiness set-point. That's fantastic news!

And here's even more great news. You don't have to sacrifice success to be happy. I'm not suggesting that it's bad to have nice things or achieve our goals in life. I'm all for that. It's just that most people have it backwards—they think that success will bring happiness. It's actually the other way around—happiness will bring more success.

I think getting older is phenomenal. As we age, we realize the belief that "I'll be happier when . . ." is a myth. We've tried to find our happiness from outer things and that didn't bring us what we were looking for in a lasting way. So we start looking for and can ultimately find happiness in all the right places.

Often people ask me if I think it's selfish to want happiness—how can that help the problems of the world? My answer is that I think that being happy is the least selfish thing we can do to contribute to this world because as we become happier, we influence everyone around us. This Chinese proverb sums that idea up well:

When there is light in the soul, there will be beauty in the person.

When there is beauty in the person, there will be harmony in the house.

When there is harmony in the house, there will be order in the nation.

When there is order in the nation, there will be peace in the world.

May we each experience more happiness in our hearts and light in our souls and through that may we help create more peace on our planet.

Marci Shimoff
Professional Speaker, #1 NY Times Best-Selling Author, Happy for No Reason, Love for No Reason, Chicken Soup for the Woman's Soul, Featured Teacher in The Secret
www.MarciShimoff.com

Follow Your Gut

I have always been an optimist. Maybe because I was lucky enough to grow up in a stable, middle class family in which people (my parents) loved what they did for a living. Maybe because I was brought up in a very special city, Florence, Italy, where one is surrounded by beauty and every corner, every street is a work of art one cannot but feel uplifted by. Or maybe it is the sunshine and the blue sky, or a combination of all this and more.

Whatever the case, I always felt and was told by mother that as a woman I needed to spread my wings and fly. "Work hard, be independent, decide what you want to be and go for it", that is what I can remember her telling me from the age of eleven or twelve. So I did or at least, I tried!

As a young university student I always dreamt of working for the European Commission; politics, international relationships and the idea of working for the greater good fascinated me. My interest in purpose as well as profit was born then, as much as the desire to make an impact and reach out to many. Eventually I went to Brussels but did not stay there for long.

London had already gained a special place in my heart and I decided to follow my gut, another recurrent theme in my personal and professional story! So I went back to the UK. Thanks to my Brussels contacts I found an entry job in an international organisation and spent the following four years travelling the world, lobbying governments, attending some very powerful gatherings, including the World Economic Forum in Davos, India, and Africa. Thanks to an inspiring president who acted as my mentor, I worked my way up to Assistant Director.

At the time I did not realise the place that mentoring was going to have in my life. Nor did I realise that he was my mentor, but by 29 I had had dinner with Simon Peres of Israel and his Palestinian "counterpart" Arafat. I had shared a flight to Namibia with Michael Jackson. I had sat a few seats away from actress Jane Fonda and her husband Ted Turner. In this pre-social media era I learnt about the power of communication. I understood the importance of engaging the audience through an inspirational vision. Perhaps most importantly I appreciated the critical importance of nurturing win-win, long term, and sustainable relationships. Much of my recent business is the result of people I met all those years ago; people who liked me and trusted me then and still do today.

Professional services were to be my next stop, working for one of the big advisory firms as consultant, industry expert, and spokesperson. In that organisation more than ever before I understood that "it is all about people." I also began to appreciate concepts such as authentic leadership and gender parity (or the lack of it). Through the work I did in industry I developed a passion for supporting women in the work place. In 2004 I launched my first business helping companies to tap into the entire talent pool, not just the male half. Mentoring, coaching, management development, networking through the first ever female awards in tourism sat at the heart of the business. This very same passion holds my second business, Everyday Mentor, which I founded in 2011—together today. Everyday Mentor is devoted to helping companies realise their people potential for better performance and greater profit. It also helps individuals—women especially but also men and across every industry—shine at whatever they wish to do personally and professionally.

I love what I do and this is what drives me out of bed every morning. At times it has been very difficult: the recession almost killed my first business; gender was an unusual topic to bring to a business table in the early noughties and before I could make a living I had to educate possible clients about the very basics.

Owning a micro-business can also feel pretty lonely at times. But the smile on the face of an empowered female manager, that "eureka" moment on the face of a coaching client; the email sent to say "what you did changed my life", repays me for every discomfort by a factor of hundred. So I am still an optimist, but living, loving, working and aging bring a certain amount of realism too. If you are thinking of launching your own business, maybe venturing out of a sound corporate job, do remember the following (because as Churchill once said, "I do not have the time to make all the mistakes myself, I have to learn from those who did them before me."):

1. Follow your gut when it comes to choosing what to do as only love and belief in your product or service can support you through the inevitable tough times ahead.

2. Plan, review, research. Guts are fine, but be sure to understand how you are going to go about your business

and, depending on your personal circumstances, think carefully whether to leave your corporate job.

3. Network, network, and network again. By this I mean develop strong, genuine relationships with people; follow up business meetings; be sincerely interested in others.

4. Give as well as take. There is no doubt what goes around comes around and I have found that thoughtful generosity is always repaid.

5. Find a mentor or two or more. There are many people out there who are keen to give back and give their time to passionate people. We can learn an awful lot from these people and at the same time we can find a safe space to discuss our concerns, find a sounding board for our ideas, or identify unexpected options. Don't worry about not being good enough for a mentor. They will learn almost as much from you as you will from them!

Finally by all means remember to be yourself. At this point in your life as a woman you are at your most confident, self-assured, and wise. In other words, a sure winner!

Alessandra Alonso, MBA
Qualified and Certified Coach-Mentor
www.Everydaymentor.co.uk

Liberate Your Rebel Spirit

Growing up, there were three things a woman could possibly aspire to be: a mother, a nurse, or a teacher. That was the pathway I was headed down but then it happened. We had a Revolution of peace, love, and freedom of expression—the 60s. I stopped wearing dresses and acting like a lady much to my high school principal father's chagrin. Instead I opted for faded blue jeans, long strait hair, and macramé necklaces. I felt liberated and free to be whatever my heart desired. So of course I chose something my father would never approve of . . . I became an artist.

My rebel, renegade, and revolutionary self was on the road to the big unknown and loving it! I set about making up my own rules, dreaming big, and exploring all the possibilities. I did all the things a young lady shouldn't do: travelled alone, went to school in Europe, and let my freak flag fly.

"I've never followed The Rules, I never have, and never will," became my Rebel Yell.

Growing up at the beach in Southern California I never considered living anywhere away from all that gorgeous nature and beautiful beaches. But when I hear someone say, "You can't do that" well, that's my cue, "Just watch me". It was 1980 when I woke up to the city that never sleeps. New York, New York: so nice they named it twice. However, it felt more like Gidget goes to Hell.

"OMG, I hate it!" Every day I woke up thinking "What am I doing here?" It was a replay of the Joni Michelle lyrics . . . "wanta see the folks I dig, even kiss a Sunset pig, California I'm coming home". And of course "The City", as the frenzied inhabitants know it, becomes a drug. It gets in your blood and you go off on a fascinating adrenaline high and so did I, for twenty-five years.

I love New York! I am living in the best city in the world, best job in the world, with the best people in the word, and I am on top of the world! That's what was going through my head that crisp clear September day walking briskly up Fifth Avenue. Yeah, my winding path, pursuing an art career, lead me to having the "it job" with all the power and glamor that "It" stands for; being an Art Director at Vogue Magazine where the devil really does wear Prada. I was living the "Sex in the City" dream.

As I came out of that Fifth Avenue chic coffee store, latte in hand going off to the subway, a group of people were on the corner staring up at the sky. As I approached my stomach started to twist. I stopped dead in my tracks and turned to see what they were looking at, just in time to see the first plane crash into the World Trade Center. "This must be an accident, what happened?" I just starred at the black hole trying to wrap my brain around what my eyes had witnessed seconds before.

When the second plane hit and the hair went up on the back of my neck, my knees started shaking as the huge ball of flames rose up into the air. "No, no, no this can't be happening; no one could survive that amount of heat". My heart was racing uncontrollably. I wanted to run but my feet were frozen, embedded in the sidewalk and my eyes fixated on the unthinkable. As I watched in horror the buildings started to fall and the tears started flowing down my face.

I was at the top of my career. I had made it! Everything that I thought was so important: being the "it girl" working at Vogue, my pursuit of power, prestige, and my art career, all just melted away. None of it mattered anymore.

What the hell was I doing? It could all be gone tomorrow in a cloud of smoke. In that moment my life changed forever. My DNA transformed from it's all about me to it's all about We. One hundred and fifty friends and colleges were gone forever. The 911 phone calls just kept playing over and over in my head with the voices saying, "I love you" and then just the eternal silence.

WTF. Where's the focus? What really matters? What am I going to do now? I sat for hours wondering, "What is my real purpose here?" It was a painful awareness that our next breath is not promised.

My whole life had been about striving to get to the top . . . hustle, and grind to get the gold ring of prestige and accomplishment. I thought that was my life's purpose. If being the "It Girl" was no longer it, then what?

I knew I had to change so I plunged headfirst into experiential learning, growth, and development and deep spiritual work. I started to see that there is a thread, a pattern of historical DNA that runs through my life. And it runs through your life too, because in truth we are all the same —*The Heart Wants to be Seen and the Soul Wants to be Connected.*

In that moment it became crystal clear that I wanted to help people, but how? I thought about all the people in those towers and wondered how many were still afraid to break free to fulfil their dreams and passions. So many of their gifts and unique talents would never be realized. What are you going to do with your one precious life?

I made a decision to bring all of myself, my heart, and creative vision to help people who have a calling to build a business that aligns with their heart. I would help them live their message and be fully self-expressed so they can make the impact they are here to make. To me it's simply about connecting and sharing the love by helping people to find their true voice.

It's smart to fit in . . . but it's brilliant to stand out.

Ann Bennett
Founder of Ann Bennett Marketing, a Speaker, Author, Coach, and Brand Profit Builder
http://annbennettmarketing.com/

Digging My Story

When I was at school in the 1970s, career options for girls were limited: teacher, nurse, or secretary. I didn't want to go to university and wasn't the Florence Nightingale type so the first two options were quickly ruled out. Learning secretarial skills appealed to me because they were practical and would guarantee a job.

I wasn't particularly ambitious—I just wanted to be financially independent. So I found myself a comfortable position as a secretary in the Civil Service, working for kindly old scientists at the Department of the Environment.

So far, so boring. But I also sang backing vocals in a moderately successful pub-rock band, which was a bit more interesting. And it was because I thought it would help to promote the band (spoiler: it didn't) that I applied to become the secretary to the *Editor of Sounds,* one of the big three music weeklies.

The atmosphere at the offices of a rock paper couldn't have been more different from the Civil Service. I was catapulted into a chaotic, exciting world when anarchy was still firmly present in the UK.

I started going out with one of Sounds' staff writers. I used to help him write reviews of new bands such as Blondie, U2, Talking Heads, and Television. Then, one day, he announced that he didn't have time to write a particular gig review and asked me to do it instead. I didn't think the editor would accept a review written by a secretary, but he did. All of a sudden I was a published writer.

I wrote for Sounds for a year while I was still a secretary. Then my boss offered me a staff writer's job. He had to fight on my behalf because the publisher we worked for believed that secretaries should know their place. But he stuck to his guns, and I got the job.

So I became the accidental music journalist. I went from being chained to a typewriter in an office typing letters and memos to being chained to a typewriter in an office writing reviews and interviews (a much better quality of chain). Oh, and I also travelled the world at record companies' expense to go on the road with various bands.

I was the first music journalist to secure an interview with Spandau Ballet—coining the term the "New Romantics" in the process—and also wrote the first published interviews with bands such as Duran Duran, Depeche Mode, and Soft Cell.

This was the start of a 15-year career in music journalism, during which time I became the editor of a pop magazine called *Record Mirror* and also worked for *New Musical Express*. It was a charmed life in many ways. I was fortunate enough to be trained on the job to become a sub-editor, headline writer, commissioning editor, and manager.

So when a former colleague made me an offer I couldn't refuse in 1993, I was ready. I left the crazy music business behind and got myself a proper job on Fleet Street – working on a new magazine supplement for *The Observer* newspaper.

Three years and 12 magazine awards later, I found my way to *The Sunday Telegraph*, where I became an assistant editor.

There must have been something I liked about Sundays, because after that I started working part-time for *The Sunday Express*. The rest of my week was spent writing a memoir of my time as a music journalist, a book that sadly still hasn't been published.

It was in the mid-Noughties that I realised I had ticked all the boxes in my career as a journalist. I'd been into personal development for many years and felt drawn to train as some kind of coach or therapist. In 2009 I found the course I'd been looking for: human potential coaching, a holistic type of life coaching created by Dr Mark Atkinson.

I graduated at the age of 54, all set to reinvent myself as a human potential coach. I was determined to leave journalism behind, especially as the hacking scandal had made me feel ashamed to call myself a journalist. I soon realised, however, that I was a drop in the life-coach ocean.

I joined a community called Inspired Entrepreneur, run by Nick Williams, author of *The Work We Were Born to Do*. He pointed out that I was in danger of throwing out the baby with the bathwater, i.e., a whole bank of valuable transferrable skills that I'd built up during my years in journalism.

Could I teach people how to spot a good story? Write a headline? Yes, and yes. Then might I consider combining that with my coach training and coming up with a unique offering? Yes please!

And thus it was that *The Story Archaeologist* was born. I now typically work with female entrepreneurs who are doing the work they love but are struggling to communicate their passion. I help them dig for the stories from their own lives that connect them not only to their sense of purpose but also to potential clients.

Two years ago I co-launched a storytelling event in central London where ordinary people could share their extraordinary stories with an audience. "The Story Party" is still going strong and is now branching out to other parts of the UK as well as abroad.

What I've realised is that I've always loved telling stories and am lucky enough to have been paid to do so. But now I have a deeper purpose, which is to help people form more meaningful connections in our disconnected digital age. And I believe story is the way to do that.

It has been an amazing journey—one that I could never have predicted when I left school at 18 with my shorthand and typing certificates. But every skill I have acquired is still serving me, serving my clients, and serving my community. And there's no such thing as an accident.

Beverley Glick
Story Archaeologist, Public Speaker, Coach and Trainer, Writer and Editor.
Read all about it at beverleyglick.com

Bridging the Gap

"What does a person do when their worlds collide?" This was the challenge I faced as I entered my middle years. I'd operated in two very different worlds, my professional or public world and my personal or private one. I was really successful at existing in both of these environments at the same time. Until I wasn't.

For over 25 years I operated as a highly successful financial executive, which as you can guess was a very logical, linear, left-brained world. At the same time I was extremely intuitive and spiritually connected to a point of seeing spirits and communing with all manner of Angels and Guides. I knew things that people deemed unknowable!

These worlds were diametrically opposed and my existence in both simultaneously created an enormous amount of stress in my life. Something had to give. Playing in the creative, connected world fed my soul. Yet my mundane career paid the bills and put my kids through university. Tough to choose!

As often happens in life, the choice was made for me. It was like my higher guidance lost patience and forced the issue. I experienced small signs that things needed to change. I needed to change. However, I became very adept at ignoring these gentle nudges offered by the Universe, leaving them no option but to pull out the BIG BAT.

After resisting the gentle shifts and holding on to my status quo for far too long, I found myself out skiing on a gorgeous winter day. I have to admit, I was strongly encouraged to sit still and process the impact of certain events occurring in my life at the time. My solution was to get moving fast enough that I could ignore them. The "BIG BAT" was delivered in the form of a tumble down a mountain, and not just any old mountain. I chose one of the biggest mountains in the Rockies for this performance.

The result of this fall from grace was about three years of down time, the first spent as my body disintegrated before me and the next two were invested in rebuilding. At my lowest point I could only be out of bed for about four hours a day and any type of activity was near impossible. To walk across my condo (about 14 meters) I had to rest half way. I went up and down the stairs on my butt for two years. Most of my days were spent on the couch watching television and healing.

Rock bottom was a very dire place for me. My once strong and fit physical body no longer operated as I had become accustomed to. With the breakdown of every system, my body chemistry was totally out of whack and that had a significant impact on the way my brain functioned. After years of processing numbers as a way of life I found myself unable to add 2 and 2 together, even with a calculator! This sent me into a tailspin emotionally with a lot of time spent in "woe is me" energy. And let's not forget the spiritual impact. I was so angry with God, my Angels, my Guides, and whoever else I could blame that I refused to connect with any form of higher guidance. All aspects of my being crumbled at the same time and life didn't seem worth living.

My true recovery began when I surrendered my victim mentality and released control of the process. The journey back was incredible. Once I became strong enough to rise from the couch I got the urge to paint. Not walls, not the kitchens or living rooms. I chose to paint pictures, which was very bizarre as I hadn't held a paint brush in my entire adult life. Under my new "no resistance" agreement with myself I sought out an art teacher and I learned to paint. I proved to have a bit of a talent for it too. It surprised me along with everyone else in my life. I found opening the creative juices that had been bottled up for a lifetime to be beyond cathartic. It was a profound blessing.

Thirty paintings later, which took most of a year, I found a new source of inspiration welling up from deep within me. Something that had never been strongly present in my life to this point. I wanted to be of service.

What did that even mean? It had no place in the world of high finance, the world that I had grown up in. And how do I support myself in this new energy of "in service". As the journey proceeded, and as I evolved, the focus on cash flow took on less and less energy and I began to explore what it meant for me to be in service to the people around me.

The word "Bridge" kept creeping into my consciousness. "I am a bridge." This is a term I often used to describe what I did in the corporate world. I was involved in what I termed "rescue and recovery" work. I took dysfunctional organizations and helped bring them to a more functional place. I helped entrepreneurs with new ideas create a structure within which to grow. A bridge was not a term that I understood outside of that context.

How can I be a bridge in this new world? What does this even mean? I took these questions with me into meditation and into sleep. They stayed with me all day every day. And clarity began to emerge.

The four fundamental areas of life, physical, mental, emotional, and spiritual, must be balanced and work in sync. This is what creates balanced momentum. I have rebuilt all of these aspects of my life twice, pulling my life out of devastation and turning it into something beautiful. I know the process. I have the resources to guide people experiencing challenges in any of these areas. With my new role clarified, my world shifted once again and I gave birth to the "Return On Integrity" project.

"Integrity" What is this? People use this term loosely resulting in ambiguity. Think back to your school days when you learned about integers—whole numbers as opposed to fractions. This is the root of integrity, wholeness. Through Return On Integrity I support people to rediscover their wholeness and create themselves as complete, entire, undiminished beings. This is where you discover your brilliance and tap into an incredible source of personal power.

This is when my life began again.

———————————

Brenda Jacobson
Supporting people to bridge the gap between their current challenges and the life of their dreams.
Website – www.brendaljacobson.com
Facebook–facebook.com/Brenda.jacobson.8
Twitter–@wolfwindgroup
Linked In–www.linkedin.com/in/brendajacobson

Heeding the Song of Your Soul

The signs were always there—some blazing fires with huge smoke plumes, some soft as pillow whispers during the night. I know this: *Whenever and however we witness the "signs of our soul calling,"* it is best to heed the call from this highest aspect of *ourselves;* that which beckons for the unique, exquisite expression of our soul and personality blended together in the world.

After a 25 year career owning three different businesses and working for a top university and several non-profit organizations, I continue to divest myself of more pieces of "who I think I should be" and am consciously creating an outward life that authentically reflects who I am inward. I have cultivated diverse skills: marketing and communications, public relations, graphic design, fundraising, event creation, promotion and production, executive management, program development, and running a business from A to Z. I am a mom to three children from two marriages and a classical soprano, dotting the decades with performances and creative collaborations.

I easily recall myriad instances of making career and life decisions laced with self-betrayal including whom I married, that I even got married, continually "climbing the corporate ladder," buying into choices that fed the illusion of financial security, but deadened my heart. The list goes on, as does the list of corresponding, escalating crises that illuminated how far out of alignment I was with my integrity.

Today, I am selling a big house that is a lingering symbolic remnant of material and career success, accumulation, and consumption; and trading it for a 504 square foot cabin and 97 acres of pristine Adirondack mountain wilderness. I am honouring the earthy goddess within; listening to the wandering traveller I know myself to be, and excavating more of the creative muse burgeoning inside. I am following the joy in my heart leading me to create a "spiritual adventure sanctuary" and "micro-momentary communities" for those who feel drawn to come.

Seven years ago, after a devastating depression, health crisis, and political intrigue that were destroying my stability and wellness on all levels, I departed from an executive position at one of the most venerable non-profits on our globe where I was gaining national recognition and accolades for my contributions. I had convinced myself that this organization was "spiritual enough" as it served so many in dire need. (My life's purpose is immersion in the Divine and "call to congregation," so to measure activities by this yardstick made sense to me.) Even after this Universal wallop, I bargained yet again by opening a communications firm that supported businesses devoted to uplifting humanity. But, the still, small voice kept whispering, "What about you? What about your wisdom? Your teachings? Your art? Your tribe waiting for you?"

When we try to be someone we are not, we are the ones who suffer. Fortunately, when we are out of alignment with our purpose, we will get indicators from the Universe. I see it like this: First, we get feather wisps across the cheek. Then, perhaps a few slaps across the face. Finally, because we are so diverted from our soul path and lost in the illusion of societal constructs, we experience a two-by-four crashing across our skull. This might look like a job loss, a divorce, a sudden and severe health crisis, or all of the above. *This extreme action is in the highest service to get across the message that we are not in alignment with our heart and soul.* We are not living passionately, purposefully, and in service.

How do we recognize our passion and purpose?

You find yourself doing something naturally, easily, without prodding. It brings you joy. You forget time. You may not think of it as important, but our *dharma* (our essential nature and purpose of incarnation) matters not whether we are an accountant, bus driver, stay-at-home parent, CEO, nun, etc. When we are in our purpose, a state of joy, gratitude, and engagement naturally arises and we radiate LIGHT, vitality, and love. This brings immeasurable benefit to ourselves, families, friends, colleagues, even strangers on the street. *The measure of a life well lived is one where we SHINE.* It is as simple as that. Each of us has a contribution, a part to play in the cosmic symphony that only we can fulfil. If we do not shine and play, something is missing in the cosmic song.

The expression of our unique soul song is not static. Just because you have broken one mould and are starting something new, do not think that "this is it." Be vigilant! Do not trade one gilded cage for another. As we consciously journey through life, we shed layer upon layer, and new aspects of our splendour arise as they are uncovered. These aspects may call for a totally new expression and manifestation of "what you do."

For years, I tried to be someone I simply was not. This is true for each of us. We are enculturated from birth into belief systems telling us: what we should want, do, be, and have, how we should feel, how we should look, who we should associate with, what we should eat, and what to believe about a God, our world, each other, and ourselves. It is part of being human. We continue to be bombarded with powerful messages tamping us down and lulling us to forget who we are. This indoctrination flows from one generation into another until we awaken and begin to ask the right questions.

Currently, I express my soul's song as wife, mom, teacher and mentor, sound and energy healer, soprano, cook, adventurer, friend, and entrepreneur. I do not try to be these things. They naturally arise from the alignment of my heart, mind, and soul working in concert. I am less attached to the expectations of those around me and more importantly, the expectations of who I believe myself to be. My essential qualities remain rooted—mystical, probing, visionary, kind, joyful, mischievous, creative, vibrant, sensual. And I trust that everything I need is already within me.

I awake each morning with wonder and gratitude. This was not always true. I feared dying, and through an undiagnosed medical condition, I was in fact, dying. I knew it intuitionally. *Everything changed the moment I realized that I dreaded dying because inherently I knew my entire life had been a waste.* If I left the planet, I would have so much of my soul song left unexpressed. So much joy, laughter, and love to share—still trapped within me. Now I have one criterion for each day: In some way, am I expressing my passion, joy, and light? That moment, that day. *I have learned I am my best and blessed when I take one breath and one step. Then begin again.*

You already know deep within you who you are, what essential soul qualities you embody. You cannot negate the burning fires or the whispers in the night that your soul speaks to you. Dive within, begin the journey to your "big S" Self. It is a journey unparalleled in adventure, awe, frustration, fright, and ultimate fulfilment. Do not try to be anything to anyone anymore. Do not play by others' rules, and most of all, break YOUR rules—the limiting beliefs you unconsciously took on.

The greatest gift you can give the world is the self-permission to be who you truly are.

————————

Christine Powers
Soprano, Activator, Teacher, and Speaker
http://www.christinepowers.com/

Embrace Change— Embrace Life

Once upon a time there was a little girl who lived in a fantasy world—or at least, she realised that's what it was when she grew up. In this world, people floated about in kaftans, drinking, and smoking, sat around on film sets made up to the hilt, pounded the stage spouting Shakespeare, or gossiped in the BBC bar after dark. In this world, no one "worked". They acted, they performed, they sang and danced, and they dressed up.

Then one day, the little girl became an adult, and realised there was a real world out there that she had to engage with. That little girl was me. But it took me a very long time to realise that I couldn't be a part of the world in which I had grown up, where my mother was an actress and my father a producer. Most people had to study, to work, to earn, and not to sing in Mecca dance halls and expect to make a living.

So finally in my thirties I got a degree and a post graduate qualification in law. I couldn't make work life balance work at the Bar, with two young children, so it took me a while to find a career that I loved, which I did in my forties, in the voluntary sector. I was happy there for many years, but post-recession, fundraising was tough, and in my late fifties I needed a change of direction.

Sessions with a life coach were incredibly helpful, and focusing on my skills and experience garnered in the charity sector, I set up my event planning business. Why event planning? Because I love helping people celebrate, seeing them happy and having a good time. I see my life purpose as creating an environment for people to enjoy themselves, to connect, to let their hair down, and, I guess, I am almost coming full circle, back to the world I grew up in, but in a more grounded way. I'm taking my mother's acting skills and my father's producing abilities and putting them together to create fabulous events.

But how was I going to get clients? Having found a local networking group, I gave myself a deadline to get my website and business cards up and running, so I could arrive fully formed at my first meeting. And that was my first mistake—I hadn't realised that you could rock up not being entirely sure of what you were doing, but would have the support of your group to get going. So that would be my tip number one: join a networking group where you will be able to get support, encouragement, and business tips from live people rather than books, which for me have been invaluable.

By Christmas that year, having blogged my heart out, I had no clients, but in late December, like buses, three came along at once! Finally, I was up and running. The first event I organised, in April, went really well, and more importantly, I enjoyed it! But business was slow, so I had to look for other opportunities I could run in tandem with the events business. And that's what's so exciting about a new career, and being self-employed: You can not only be alive to new opportunities, but you can actually go for them and grab them by the whatsits!

So the middle of 2015 saw me going back to my old charity for a three-month campaign, not in fundraising but in communications. And how I loved it! Writing persuasive copy, talking to business organisations, producing films, even giving radio interviews—all playing to my strengths. Most importantly, I found my writing mojo during that three-month stint. How? Because I had to write an evaluation report on the campaign, which ran to over 5,000 words. It had been ages since I had written such a tome, and it made me realise that I could write what would have been a dry report in an engaging and informative style.

Buoyed up with this rediscovered skill, I decided to write a book about event planning, which took me just four weeks to put together. Writing the book has given me the support I need when imposter syndrome strikes. This is something so many people feel, but particularly affects solopreneurs. Now I have the written word—my written word—which evidences my knowledge of the event business, and that makes me feel much more secure when I pitch to clients.

Working on your own can be a lonely business, but I've realised that when I'm not on site or talking to clients, I actually love sitting at my PC and writing. I look forward to the cocoon that is my little office at the top of the house where I can create, plan, and manage my business, whether it's through blogging, social media, or marketing.

So where am I now, eighteen months on? Business is still slow, and I have had to take on other small projects to keep the wolf from the door, but having a portfolio of careers is something I would never have dreamed of a few years ago. It's something that women over 40 can and should embrace. And my tip number two is—be brave! The wonderful thing about getting older is that you become less worried about what people think. Of course you have to be mindful of your potential clients, but if you are clear about the type of clients you want to work with, you can be confident because you can be yourself—and you can be who you want to be, because you've left behind the baggage of your years of employment. As Simon Sinek, the business guru, says, "People buy why you do it," so if you're clear about why you do what you do, you'll get the clients you want to work with.

I love my life now. I loved it before, but that previous life has given me the tools to enjoy this one. So embrace change, embrace life, and be yourself: how lucky is that!

Deborah Granville
Founder and Director of DezEvents.com. Author of <u>Fabulous Functions for the Faint-Hearted</u>

If Not Now—When?

I think my entrepreneurial spirit has always been there although it definitely didn't come from my family. I was brought up to think that I should get a good job and not take any chances. I have always loved being creative and my working life started with a job in the art department of a department store creating layout designs for advertising. I married young but then tragedy struck. My husband died and I was a widow at 20.

I then trained to be a florist, eventually owning my own florist shop. I remarried and had two wonderful children. My creativity then moved me to work for a newspaper as a paste-up artist. Computers were just coming into use and I soon was adept at composition and started my graphic design career. I always did other things on the side, partly to bring in extra income and partly to satisfy my entrepreneurial spirit. Through network marketing, I sold children's clothes, children's books, and skin care products.

I was in my 40s and, sadly, my 15 year marriage was not working out. And then I discovered that I had a large tumour on my spine and I had to spend three weeks in hospital having it removed. While I was recovering I had a lot of time to think.

After everything I had been through I decided to end my marriage. Within a few weeks I had no marriage, no job, no car, and I had to sell my house and move my children away from their neighbourhood. Oh, and I was wearing a back brace! It was time to take action and do something different in my life. I signed up for a personal development course even though I could barely cover the cost. I was in a state of total surrender. My friends were worried by my total certainty that everything was going to be okay.

The course peeled away layers and got to the essence of me, who I really was. I discovered that I was a strong, something that I had covered up for so long. I started to rebuild.

At that point everything changed. I was offered a job as a graphic designer for a union. A car showed up and I received some money through an inheritance. The support and the money started to flow. I loved the work but after a while I felt restless and trapped in a 9 to 5 existence. I realised that as well as the design work I was spending part of my time coaching and counselling the colleagues who showed up at my office door. I got satisfaction from working with them and helping them. What I was doing was so much more than graphic design.

Having worked for other people for 30 years I wanted to take a year off to reflect on the future and try ideas I had been playing with. I was in a supportive relationship with man I am now married to, so it was the perfect time to spread my wings. I started a graphic design company, Creative On the Move, which evolved into event planning, a magazine, and the base of the Fabulous@50 brand.

In 2007 I was 49 and I started to write a blog about what it meant to turn 50. I was feeling disconnected from people. I had been focussing on survival and bringing up my kids. I wanted to explore women's feelings. In 2008 I formed Fabulous @50 to inspire, educate, and empower women in midlife by bringing them together virtually and in person to network, share, care, and grow. It started as a local meet-up group and grew quickly. I developed a website and after two years I had a trade show. From that, I saw the business potential of my vision.

I started the group, not just for a place to meet other women, but to be inspired by other women, to grow, and, most of all, to move forward, letting go of the crap we women manage to carry around and finding something new to feel excited about being in this age of transformation. Although the underlying intent is serious, we also have a lot of fun. I believe that if you can learn to laugh about the foibles of menopause or marriage, aging and aching, you're half way to accepting them and getting on with your life.

The Fabulous@50 trade show has been dubbed a Martini Experience and includes exhibits ranging from designer purses to Botox to belly dancing. But in the midst of the bling, there's also serious information about health, finances, investments, and personal development.

Early this year, 2016, saw the publication of my book, *The Fabulous@50 Re-Experience*. It started with the blogs and then I worked with a documentary writer who did all of the research. Writing was such a learning process. I have had so many wonderful experiences in the last 10–15 years. It has been like a university education. I have developed an inspirational talk based on the principles of the book which I love presenting. Eventually I will create workshops.

It is never too late to follow your dreams and be passionate about life. I am clear now about my purpose in life. I want to build a community of women across Canada to help women to come together and support each other, and encourage continuous learning and growth. Women are about so much more than the roles they have been allocated by society.

I am grateful for my strengths. I see the gifts in other people, even when they don't see them themselves. I make people feel comfortable and I am sensitive towards people's needs. Like a lot of women I have had to overcome feelings around "Who do you think you are?" "Don"t get too big for your britches." I look for answers and don't accept "that's just the way it is." I will persevere.

Everything has led to what I do now. I feel that I am divinely led to do what I am doing. The people around me and my relationships are very important. I value being honest, transparent, and open, and being able to listen to my inner wisdom. There are lots of women looking for role models and I hope I am one. I want to show them the possibilities.

Through all of my experiences I have known that I am a strong person. There isn't anything I can't deal with.

My best advice to women becoming midlife entrepreneurs is to associate with like-minded people at your own level of development or higher. Don't seek advice from people who will give you fear-based answers. You only need feedback that comes from a place of understanding.

Make space for what you most want to do. Remember, you don't have to do everything yourself. It may take time but it is important to build a great support system.

And don't overthink it—just get started!

Dianna Bowes
abulous@50 Founder – CEO, Creative Director
2015 Winner of Stevie Award, Bronze—Female Entrepreneur of
the Year in Canada
2014 Business Leaders of Tomorrow Award
2014 Winner of Stevie Award, Gold—Best Event and Bronze,
Women Helping Women
2011 YWCA Women with Distinction—Turning Point Category
www.fabulousat50.com

The Accidental Entrepreneur

I am an accidental entrepreneur!

Life unfolded perfectly to lead me down that path—but I didn't head that way knowingly. If you'd have told me years ago that one day I would have my own successful wellness business that I ran from home, on my own terms, I would have thought you were delusional!

I was born to help people, an awareness that came to me early in life; however it has taken an extremely convoluted pathway to get to the point where I feel totally happy with how that gift has evolved into a life/business that truly serves others, whilst honouring me too.

I left school without the qualifications I was capable of, preferring partying and "fitting-in" to studying. I was a typical rebellious teenager, leaving home against my parents' wishes, aged 18, with barely any money, a decent home, or any concrete plans.

I started my career path the hard way, letting stubbornness and a desperate need for independence lead me. Thankfully, my inner "sensible" parental programming was deeply installed, so I eventually started a nursing diploma, only to hurt my back so badly 18 months later that I was advised to discontinue.

Five years of soul-searching followed; looking for "life" answers, surviving on my wits, earning minimal money, doing dull jobs, until the day a young friend died, and I truly woke up. I distinctly remember hearing a voice in my head that day, saying, "Would I feel cheated if I died tomorrow?"

I realised I had been gifted life, skills, and intelligence and owed it to myself to use them, so I started exploring what I loved and was good at. Having "coasted" up to that point, this marked my first conscious "head over heart" decision, one that later taught me that the heart always wins out in the end!

What I wanted was an English degree—but at age 25, having lived independently for 7 years, I chose a vocational radiography degree because I knew it guaranteed an income, meaning I could pay the bills whilst also helping people. It never occurred to me back then that there was any other way to earn a living than to be employed by a "reliable" organisation such as the NHS.

It wasn't long before I became disillusioned—feeling like I worked in a human conveyor belt—and whilst I endeavoured to treat people like people (rather than a "broken arm casualty"), it was hard to always honour that in a frantic environment. I saw people for who they truly were, regardless of what they presented with, and I learned that treating them well helped them see that too, something about that really resonated with me.

A seed was sown . . .

In my drive to "find my thing" and help people like I wanted to, I specialised in ultrasound; thinking it would give me more autonomy and "connection" time. Long story short—it didn't!

Around this time, I met the man who subsequently became my husband, as well as my rock, champion, and guide. Meeting him changed my life. At age 30, for the first time in my life, I had an equal partnership, one where we both helped each other to become better versions of ourselves.

He helped me see that I was motivated by helping people to shine, and fate conspired to let this unfold. Not long into my ultrasound career and marriage, it became apparent that parenthood wasn't our destiny, and after several miscarriages and failed IVF, I had to honour my heart and walk away from a job that saw me breaking my heart and compromising my values daily.

This was my second wake-up call. This time I followed the path without any idea or expectations about where it would lead. I knew I wanted to continue helping people and didn't want to waste the knowledge I had. So I opted to train in Shiatsu, which seemed to combine both, whilst also enabling me to treat clients respectfully.

Thus began a more conscious path, where I started listening to my inner guidance. Alongside Shiatsu, I began practising yoga and meditation, reading self-development books, clearing old traumas, and rediscovering my inner self. I set up my practice, working 1-to-1 helping people address whatever they presented with, whilst continuing to study whatever curiosity led me towards.

This worked well. I loved it and my clients loved it. My practice grew through word-of-mouth and I was booked weeks in advance, but when I had to undergo a hysterectomy aged 42, I was forced to face the fact that I couldn't continue working at the same rate, as I was burnt out.

Fate steps in when things need changing, by "gifting" me healing time, it also gave me a well-timed practice pause. By now I knew that my superpower was helping women find inner calm and rediscover their inner light. What I hadn't realised was how hard it was to do that if I continued to work like I was my own 9–5 "employee"!

I followed the path onwards, finally seeing that I ran a business, not "just" a practice and that all of my lessons were fitting together to form a clear purpose, one that truly served others.

Now with an ongoing commitment to create sanctuary space, support, and resources to help women embody all that they already are, I have finally uncovered and embraced not only my life purpose, but also my inner entrepreneur, and I truly believe that all our experiences contribute perfectly to our unique path, even if we don't always know that at the time.

I don't know what answers you seek—but I do know they're inside you. Trust in that and hold onto your vision unapologetically, wholeheartedly, and with lightness and joy—and enjoy the unfolding journey!

Helen Rebello
Peaceful Pathfinder who provides a safe sanctuary space for heart- centred women who've lost themselves a little in serving others.
www.thetranquilpath.co.uk

JILL McCULLOCH

Back Into The Flow

The cannon blasts and we're off. Three strong strokes. Legs pushing hard, my hands start moving rapidly with the oar. The boat surges forward. My breathing is shallow. I can feel the crew keeping time with me increasing the power and speed. The boat chasing us is closing the gap, closing in on us. The cox is looking ahead and doesn't know, his eyes are on the boat we're chasing. I feel the panic rise in my chest:

"What am I doing here? I'm 48 years old, I could have a heart attack. If I have a heart attack, at least then I can stop. I'd have to die though. Die and fall out of the boat. Surviving would be unforgiveable."

How on earth did I find myself in this terrifying position? Never a sporty person, I bunked off "Games" wherever possible to rehearse something theatrical. In adult life, AmDram had kept me busy for thirty years and a number of expensive unattended gym memberships nearly had me joining the army to get fit! Yogalates, Zumba, tap dancing, salsa, I've tried them all but most were followed by a dough-nut or a visit to the pub!

Back in 2012, at forty-seven years old, married—with three children, I was struggling with menopausal symptoms. Heavily overweight, I was feeling a "bit blue" which is apparently how most "strong women" describe borderline depression. My Dad was diagnosed with lung-cancer. Marketing my coaching practice is abandoned as we spend his last seven weeks writing his memoires.

In fairness I'd spent the last five years on the touch line of my son's football and rugby matches and Tai Kwando. At twelve he was now old enough to row with my husband and youngest daughter. Finally, I was looking forward spending the weekend mornings lounging in bed with coffee, croissants, and the papers!

However, I made the mistake of seeing a life coach. Wanting more time with my rowing mad husband, I commit to a Learn to Row Course. Secretly, I thought "I'll do it and hate it but at least I will have tried."

Grudgingly I started in a single sculling boat (two oars) and loved the peace, the closeness to nature and even the exercise. Believe me, rowing exercises every inch of your body, except your scalp! Despite capsizing in early April, no-one was more surprised than I to discover I loved rowing!

Soon I took a seat in the Isle of Ely Women's Eight (that's a crew of eight rowers, one oar each and a cox). In the boat the cox instructs the direction, power, timing, and the speed of stroke. The cox's voice is the only one in the boat. Chatting is not encouraged, which people who know me find hilarious. The strain of rigidly following everyone else, keeping attention to detail and staying in complete silence was almost too much to bear. However, eventually it quietens my monkey brain and being subsumed to the will of the whole crew leaves me with an incredible sense of peace and calm. Total physical focus for ninety minutes brought home what mindfulness actually means.

My goal was to row in the Cambridge Town Bumping Races the following year, which take place over four nights every July. For the uninitiated, The Bumps are a set of historic races where eighteen Eights line up on the River Cam, a length and a half apart. A canon fires and each crew rows rapidly to catch and bump the crew in front and hopefully avoid being bumped by the chasing crew. It is not for the feint-hearted, terribly exciting to watch, and terrifying to row!

We trained over that very long winter in snow, rain, and Fen winds. Our old, patched-up Eight fell apart and we had to train in Pairs and Fours in the Spring, only borrowing an Eight for Bumps week itself.

Bumps week 2013 arrived. Little did I imagine that I would be put at Stroke (setting the pace for the crew) with two elite rowers behind me and a GB oarsman coxing in front. Weeds stuck in our rudder the first night and we almost crashed into Grassy Corner. We avoided being caught on the following two nights, despite me catching a crab and losing my seat. I refused to give up and suffered friction burns from sliding up and down on my bottom (who needs Christian Grey!) The last night arrived:

Fear has overwhelmed me. Recognising it, I breathe deeply and take back control. The crew settle into the pace with me and we pull away from the chasing boat. Our bank party are shouting and cheering us to push harder. There's one whistle, then two whistles and the cox shouts "Bumps Ten". We row for our lives, lifting ourselves out of our seats with the power of the stroke. Suddenly he shouts "Hold her up!" We stop the boat, fearing a crash into the bank, only to find we had Bumped!

Bumps was an incredible experience and huge learning: my technique and fitness improved dramatically and I dropped 30lbs and two dress sizes in 18 months, all because I wanted to be in the boat!

Competitive rowing has taught me the importance of doing your best in each moment, not just aim for the outcome. Rowing has enabled me to switch off from my circumstances, build strength, resilience, control, and the determination to just keep going: to win, to win for the crew.

Just committing to change one aspect of our lives can bring positive results across the board. Outside of my world of business, rowing gives me the joy of mixing with scientists, academics, and professionals with an entirely different outlook on life. It enabled me to overcome the grief of losing my dad. A love of rowing continues to connect me to my son, and my husband and I are now closer than we have ever been in 25 years together.

This quote from Kim Bassinger sums it up for me, *"When I'm old I'm never going to say, 'I didn't do this' or 'I regret that.' I'm going to say, 'I don't regret a damn thing. I came, I went, and I did it all.'"*

Jill McCulloch
Co-Active Coach. For more information on coaching or her rowing inspired blog see www.coachyou.co.uk

Scratching My Entrepreneurial Itch

Some entrepreneurs are born, some are made, and some of us just sort of "evolve." Me? I fall firmly into the latter camp—in fact, it took me the best part of 50 years to finally scratch my longstanding entrepreneurial itch and start a business of my own. (I'm not one to rush into things!)

I started my working life as a teacher, quite simply because it seemed the best of a bad bunch of suggestions offered by my careers advisor at the time. The other two suggestions were nursing and secretarial and, as anyone who knows me well will testify, I am eminently suited to neither! Considering this inauspicious start to my career, I actually turned out to be a pretty fine teacher and gave my very best to the some of the liveliest kids east London had to offer!

At that stage, it looked as though my career path was set out before me, but ten years down the line it reached an unscripted crossroads and I resigned—an act which those around me considered to be either brave or mad. Deep down, I knew that my love of teaching had run its course and so it was time to move on and look for new pastures.

What followed was a period I affectionately describe as my "wilderness years." Looking back now with the benefit of hindsight, I can see quite clearly that this is where it all started, the beginnings of my quest to "do something different." All I knew was that I had an unidentifiable "itch" that I couldn't quite reach but I was determined to keep trying! My efforts to do so set me off on a long and winding path via a couple of very interesting diversions and a few dead ends too along the way!

I had a heady sense of freedom, adventure, and excitement as I ventured into a world far removed from the one I knew as a teacher, on a journey which took me from kitchen designer through to company director! I felt like I'd been let loose in a shoe shop where I could try on any pair I liked the look of and although some were a more comfortable fit than others, sooner or later the pinch-points inevitably started to hurt.

I felt a dawning realisation (along with a rising panic), that somewhere along the line I had become what I termed "psychologically unemployable"! My inner voice kept repeating what I knew deep down to be the truth: I didn't want to work for someone else, I didn't want to implement other people's ideas and I certainly wasn't prepared to compromise my values any more. I wanted to do things my way, doing what I enjoyed and what I was good at! The only problem was, I didn't have a clue what that could be, or if it was even possible.

Hearing that repetitive inner voice was one thing but it took the loss of both my parents within six months of each other for me to finally listen to it. And when I did, the first action I took, for which I will be eternally grateful, was to find myself a life coach. Quite simply, this one action changed my life.

A few hours of dedicated focus helped me to not only "see" what had been staring me in the face for years but also, and most importantly, catapulted me into action in a BIG way and led me to qualify as a coach and subsequently set up in business for myself. At long last I had found a way to pull all my eclectic skills and experience together . . . at long last I found the thing I loved to do . . . MY thing.

After revelling in an initial period of euphoria, I soon realised that it wasn't enough to have a passion for what I was doing; passion without profits wasn't a business. A pivotal moment for me was when I understood and accepted that first and foremost I was a business owner and in order to do "my thing", I needed to learn how to "do" business . . . and fast!

Much to my surprise I absolutely loved learning how to "do" business but I loved helping others learn how to do it even more—once a teacher, always a teacher I guess! This led me to set up Prime Time Business, a business which not only makes my heart soar but also allows me to express my unique combination of skills, talents, and experience in an authentic, and viable way.

It is now my absolute passion and privilege to show other women in their 50s and beyond how to create businesses and lives that fit who they have become. Women who are ready for their next evolution and who simply need a guiding hand from someone who has already headed down the same path they now want to take.

Midlife is a natural time of introspection, reassessment, and evolution for many of us as we prepare to move into a new and dynamic life stage. It's a time when we seek to realign who we are with what we do and look for ways to channel our hard-won experience and talents into something which enables us to make a difference AND make a living.

Creating a business presents us with a fantastic opportunity to do all that.

Creating my business has certainly been the most challenging, exciting, rewarding, and scariest thing I've ever done. I've loved every single moment and wouldn't want to do anything else. I sometimes wish it hadn't taken me quite so long to arrive here but I also know that personal evolutions take time and follow their own schedules. I'm just grateful that I've finally managed to scratch my elusive "itch" and evolve into the person I spent a long time looking for.

———————

Karen Knott
Prime Time Business
www.primetimebusiness.co.uk

Swim!

I have always seen myself as the black sheep of the family. Born in Yorkshire, England to a working class family, I was the first of the extended family to have the privilege to go to Grammar School, on to University and achieve a degree in Social Sciences.

I worked in retail at the weekends to earn my own money from the age of 16 and found myself once again in retail management after finishing university. I hated it. I was bullied by the store manager and could not wait to find a way out.

The opportunity came 18 months later when a 20m private motor yacht sailed into Hull marina. I packed in my job and apartment and jumped on board. I never swam back. I spent the next 30 years of my life living in Mallorca, Spain. After working on boats, I started a guardianage business looking after holiday homes for the rich and famous. At one point I had 30 staff working for me. I have never worked with anyone since.

I met my husband and, shortly after, our first son was born, we bought a farmhouse that needed renovation. When number two son came along I decided to quit my housekeeping work so that I could focus on the boys. I became a work at home mum. We renovated the finca, and my new profession became one of landlady/hostess to holiday families staying in our guest house, as well as tending to organic farmland.

As the boys grew I had an epiphany one day. I realised that within the next ten years, they would be flying the nest and, with hubby involved in his own successful construction business, I would be home alone. It was on that very same day I opened a magazine and saw for the first time the words "life coach". It hit me "This is what I truly wanted to do during my empty nest years".

For the next ten years between the ages of 40-50, I trained, learned, and learned some more. The biggest work needed to be done was on myself. How could I help others if I had not grown out of my own comfort zones? I took transferable skills from my degree, sailing experiences, looking after property and guests and began working as a personal development coach. Time management, organisational effectiveness, self-motivation, good listening skills and the ability to learn and add new skills became valuable to me as I moved into an unknown world.

I loved my work but my husband suffered from bouts of depression. With parents ageing and a house full of raging hormones, I turned to blogging to write about my personal feelings. My blog was found by an acquaintance who suggested I used my writing skill to take my coaching online and Sensibly Selfish was born.

Going on-line meant taking on new skills. I found myself writing a book, building a WordPress website and gaining social media expertise. I was like a sponge and loved it all. I looked for specific support through mentors and coaches as well as attending courses and workshops. For example, my public speaking experiences began at a local Toastmasters group. I now have paid support to keep my websites in good working order.

My husband is my biggest champion and confidante. Without him I would not have carried on.

Success for me has always been about the light bulbs I see going on when someone gets that change is possible, and the goose pimples I have on my skin when I know I have made the difference to that one person. Changing lives, one by one was my motto. Yet something was missing, the cash was not flowing in enough.

2015 saw many changes in my life and another time for an epiphany. My husband was offered a job in Zanzibar. Within the space of four months, we had de-cluttered our home of 20 years and put it on the market. We moved to a two roomed house just ten minutes from a pristine tropical beach with just 20 kgs of luggage each.

I had the Internet so my work came with me and yet, with ditching so much physical and mental baggage of my own, I began to see life differently. My beliefs and values had changed. I was no longer talking about making a smaller footprint on the earth, living a simple lifestyle, eating organic fresh produce and having daily times to exercise and meditate, I was actually doing it!

With newfound space in my life, I had time to step back and look at the bigger picture. I realised that coaching was not what I truly offered. People came to me for advice, for the experiences in life I had already got the t-shirts for and, more importantly, for a confidential ear to listen to them without blame, judgement, or criticism. This year I am refocusing my work and websites to signify that change.

As I look back at the words I have typed above I feel proud of my achievements. Is there something I would change?

Yes, of course! I have always been the type of person who jumps into the deep end of a swimming pool and then realises that I still have to learn to swim in that particular pool! What follows is a series of near drownings before I eventually surface to doggy paddle and then swim. Learning new things is part of my nature yet this is not for everyone.

My advice to other midlife entrepreneurs is that you can skip a lot of "treading water" by finding others who have already done a good length or two. Take whatever help you can find, you do not need to learn every skill related to your work. Also, never be afraid to jump out of one pool and into another no matter what others may tell you. After all, at this stage of life time is precious and needs to be used well.

Kay Newton
Speaker, Author, and Confidante
www.kay-newton.com

Create Your Future

One of my favourite quotes is "The best way to predict the future is to create it," by Peter Drucker. I took this to heart and always followed my passions. I thought I knew exactly what I wanted to do and I set out on the path to create it. I never thought that I would change directions completely and start a business in an industry I knew nothing about. It was a turning point in my life that enabled me to find my true purpose and passion.

I had always had a love for magazines and writing. As a kid I would write short stories and in school the essay tests were a breeze compared to math, science, and even multiple choice. In college I majored in Radio/TV with a minor in Journalism. I did the intern path and worked for a local fitness publication where I learned the ins and outs of publishing. After graduation, I thought I was ready to conquer the New York world of magazines. I interviewed at some of the top women's magazines and Conde Nast Publishing and even US magazine only to discover that as an editorial assistant the pay was $16,000 a year. Suddenly I was wondering if I could even make a living in the publishing world.

I moved back to my home town near San Francisco and started the job process. I came across a job as an assistant for a lobbyist who specialized in land development, two things I knew nothing about but I was getting desperate for a job. I hit it off with the owner. She was a one woman powerhouse show and to this day she is the best boss I ever had. I didn't know it at the time but she was really teaching me leadership more than she was teaching a skill set. Her connections led me to two other jobs, one in PR where I was able to use my writing and marketing skills and one where I was able to create a company newsletter. Good experiences, but there was no room for growth. I needed a change and I was longing to get into the magazine world and get away from a boyfriend.

Without really thinking about it I moved to Arizona where my sister was and on a whim I called the publisher of the magazine I worked at in Tucson. It turns out she was expanding to Phoenix and looking for someone to run that office. I said yes not realizing that running it meant I was going to do everything. I learned the ropes as I went and did everything including answer the phones, schedule interviews and photographers, write articles, sell advertising, help create advertising campaigns, did the invoicing, and everything else that was needed to get the monthly publication out. I loved it. I got a taste of running my own magazine.

During that time I found that although I still had a passion for writing I really enjoyed the interaction with clients on the advertising side and it was time for me to move to a bigger magazine. I made a home at the largest magazine in Phoenix where I stayed for 6 years. I left the magazine to start a business to help teens with self-esteem. After many business plans, research development, and money I had to realize the business wasn't the time so I went back to the publishing world and found my dream job. I was publisher of a glossy resource book, ran the Arizona office and for three years loved my job, the company, and the staff I hired. And then the company ran out of money and closed.

I found my next challenge with another publishing company that had a business model I thought was smart. They had five magazine titles and had sales reps in different cities who sold advertising and provided local content. They printed it and distributed and provided national content. I was responsible for recruiting the local publishers and teaching and training them with our system. I found I really enjoyed the teaching and training. I was able to travel and help people start their own magazines. The job itself was great but the environment wasn't. The team was negative. Our boss was great at first but missed seeing the culture that was being created. The other piece that was missing for me was there was no room to grow. I was feeling stuck when my sister came to me with a business opportunity in Network Marketing.

My first reaction was absolutely not. No way. Not a chance. It was in the health and wellness industry and I wasn't interested. I didn't get the business model and thought it was all about selling products and I was tired of selling. My sister had a vision that I didn't and she understood that network marketing produces more women millionaires than any other industry. I still said "no", until one day I was just tired of being tired at work and tired of not having time to do anything else I wanted to. So I decided to learn more but I was reluctant.

What I heard surprised me. I found out the business model is based on teaching and training. It was about empowering people to live their dream life. It wasn't about selling it was about building people. I could be my own boss, work my schedule and have unlimited income opportunity. At the same time I didn't have to worry about marketing, packaging, building a website, product development, distribution, payroll or anything else that most small businesses have to do. The business model was starting to make sense. Build a network of people who are shopping for great products and teach those interested how to run their own million dollar business. I jumped and 7 months later I found myself almost matching my full time income working part time. All of a sudden I had choices. I said goodbye to corporate and never looked back!

Owning my own business has completely changed my life. I got my time back and was able to go back to some of the things I love which included writing. I co-authored my first book, *Boys Before Business:* The Single Girls Guide to Having It All, and I created a membership business for the book. I helped my husband open his first business which we recently turned into a non-profit.

I learned the importance of surrounding yourself with amazing people, people who are going to bring out the best version of you. I learned that controlling your own destiny is empowering. Having choices and time are game changers. When you are open and willing for change your path might take some twists and turns. The key is to be committed to your own personal growth and be willing to fail forward. Each experience gives you valuable information. Each job led me closer to my purpose and passion. I still love magazines but what I love more is being able to impact people's lives and help them realize their dreams.

You have to be willing to take a chance, be willing to learn as you go, be willing to quit something when it isn't fulfilling you, and surround yourself with amazing people.

Success happens when you can love what you do and love the people you do it with, and be able to make a difference.

―――――――

Kimberly Mylls
Certified Leadership Coach, Author and Co-Founder of Boys Before Business
http://www.boysbeforebusiness.com/

Creating a Fulfilling Life

I'm 47 years old, I've just resigned my job and I've no idea what I'm going to do next. All I know is I've had enough of working for someone else.

Up until this point in my life I've drifted without purpose. After leaving university I joined the UK Civil Service thinking that the Department of Environment would be a great place to use my degree in geography. Instead they make me a buyer and I spend 20 years setting up and managing contracts for the multitude of things required for government to function such as security, catering, cleaning, and carpets.

And I never really enjoy it. There are occasional moments, but there's always something missing. I stay because I've met a lovely man and the civil service is really flexible when you have children and that's what we want.

We start our quest for a family when I'm 36 and I discover that my fertility is dropping off a cliff. Over the next three years we go through six rounds of IVF and come out the other side without the child we so desperately wanted. We're not offered support or help of any kind and it feels as if we are the only people in the world who can't have children. I have no one to tell me I'm grieving; all I know is that I'm sad and have to keep it inside because telling anyone seems impossible.

I feel that there has to be more to my life than the work I do, but I stay because Mum is ill and I can't summon up the energy or enthusiasm to look for another job. A few years pass, Mum dies and I start working for a charity. I have a strong yearning to make a difference and this seems like it might be the answer. But it isn't, I hate it and I realise now this is because of the complete mismatch between their stated values and how they put them into practice. My values of honesty and fairness are also really compromised, so I resign.

So here I am, 47 years old, no job, no career, no purpose, no children, one parent dead and the other recovering from a serious illness and living 200 miles away.

It feels like a complete release—I realise that for the last seven years I've been denying the truth of my life and now I have the freedom to do what I want to do, to shape my life as I want it.

And it's scary. How DO you start again? I have no idea what I want to do, all I know is that I don't want a job anymore.

But where to begin?

A friend has learned NLP (Neuro Linguistic Programming) and I decide to give it a go. So many things slot into place and I set up a coaching business to help midlife women. And it doesn't work. Why? Because I'm not being true to myself, to my identity. I want to support childless women but doing so means owning my story I don't feel strong enough inside to do it.

Then I hear Brené Brown talk about owning your story. She says: "When you deny your story, it defines you. When you own your story, you get to write a brave new ending. You get to say it was horrible and I was in lots of pain ... and then I got help and this is how the story ends."

It's like a massive jolt, it sums up my life perfectly and I realise that I've had enough of denying my childlessness.

I realise that there's a big difference between saying "I am childless" and "we couldn't have children." My childlessness doesn't define me, but what I've been through, my life experiences and my training means I have a lot to offer others who are struggling. It feels like I've found my purpose at last. However, after spending ten years hiding from the truth of my life, being open about who I really am feels so overwhelming that I almost want to back out. But I can't because this is my purpose.

I know that I can't do this alone. It's against my whole upbringing to ask for help but I know that I need business skills and support to make this work. I find a business coach who believes in me and the difference I want to make in the world. She teaches me the skills I need to change my business to support childless women and encourages and supports me to create it in alignment with my authentic self.

Everything slots into place. For the first time in my life I know who I am and my purpose in the world, I'm working to my values and beliefs and I have the skills I need. And it's absolutely wonderful.

Three years on I've learned that the road to successful self-employment can be a rocky one and having a small group of like-minded women to pick me up after falls and celebrate my successes is invaluable.

And most importantly, being completely sure of my purpose and knowing who I am is key for me, I know that when everything is in alignment anything is possible.

———————

Lesley Pyne
Supporting childless women to heal and to create a fulfilling life.
www.LesleyPyne.co.uk

I Surrender

Like everyone else on the planet, I've faced my share of challenges and hardships. I mastered single parenting five children while juggling five part-time jobs through extremely ill health. I survived various life-threatening ailments and crises. I've endured the heartbreak of overwhelming loss and grief in various ways.

But one of the most challenging periods of my life hit me when after years of raising children or doing self-employed work that was anything but mainstream, I'd lost everything in terms of financial assets, and had to figure out how to begin again. Without a safety net. And I was in my 50s. Not the happiest time to start over, much less without a solid work history to give me even a bit of a foundation.

It also meant leaving my beloved England. After leaving Canada several years earlier and becoming a British citizen, I had intended to stay in the UK for the rest of my life. But when the economic situation blew up, I could no longer earn a living with my art, readings, or healing work.

It seemed that the only sensible choice was to return to Calgary and "set up shop" where interest in readings, alternative therapies, meditation etc. was just budding many years prior when I left for England.

But I discovered that there was so much interest after all those years that the market was completely saturated in everything I knew how to do. Even worse, many of those services were being offered free.

Making it even more difficult, I didn't know many people in Calgary any more. Any business I would create using my experience and abilities relied on a network of friends and business connections. For all intents and purposes, I had none. I was going to have to try to find a job.

The thought sickened me; I'd had decades of freedom, being my own boss, living a wonderful, creative, artistic life of travel and keeping strange hours and working so it fit around my schedule. The idea of being stuck at a desk, or selling clothes, or working in a fast food restaurant was more than I could bear.

But I didn't have much choice. I was going to have to figure this out in a hurry.

Without traditional skills and experience, I was "under qualified" for any jobs that would pay enough to support me. It didn't matter that I learn extremely quickly, that I'm hard-working and dedicated, that I had loads of people skills, could type 160 words per minute, or that I'm exceptionally creative. They couldn't care less that I'm efficient, organised, and perfectionistic about making sure the job is done properly.

I couldn't even speak with anyone in an attempt to plead my case. All phone enquiries were met with "Fill out the online form and submit your résumé."

Ah, the résumé. It was painful to try to put together decades of my unusual life and work history into something that made me look remotely professional and worth a second look. I had done the best I could with it. But it never resulted in an interested employer.

I was "over qualified" for any jobs that I could have done, such as working in a shop. Prospective employers said I would be bored silly and quit, or they suggested that I would leave them as soon as I could build a business on the side and they'd be wasting their time training me.

I had spent decades overcoming countless challenges, working steadily at healing the trauma and resulting damage from a toxic upbringing. I had loads of personal and professional experience that I'd been using to help many people for a very long time. But it didn't seem to count where employers were concerned.

I had to take the entrepreneurial route and create a business based on what I was able to do. All I really wanted to do was write, paint, and make music but all of the business and marketing experts (along with the general public) said that was impossible to do. And I chose to believe them.

So I kept shifting gears. I was going to create this or that business that would allow me to use this or that set of skills. I would have to do webinars, live training events and—oh dear Lord—"coaching." I have no problem with others who use that word but it is so not me!

None of it worked. I felt increasingly discouraged and completely lost. Terrified for my future, I supported myself with mounting debt.

I reached a point where I had to surrender to my situation—that "Let go and Let God" idea. In a tearful meditation late one evening, I contemplated the worst that could happen: bankruptcy and sleeping on friends' sofas for a few days here and there until somehow I could rebuild my life.

I didn't know how I would ever manage to create and maintain a business living like that but I understood that continuing to worry about it was only blocking the flow of energy and creativity in my life.

And I understood that as much as I wouldn't like living that way, I could do it.

So with that, I let it all go and asked to be shown what to do and where to go.

Two days later, I had three miracles in one day. Each was an answer to a very big prayer. Within the following two weeks, there were several more. The most bizarre "coincidences" and signs, one after another as though airport runway lights were turned on over the path I was meant to take.

I continued to listen and pay attention, feeling as though the universe was screaming one big fat "Yes!" at me after another.

Then came the biggest, brightest idea I had ever had in my life. I was dumbfounded when there it was in front of me: It was the perfect combination of my art, writing, and music with my abilities to empower people to transform their lives.

Even better, it had nothing to do with webinars or "coaching" and it had everything to do with me getting to package up the most important aspects of who I am and what I have to offer, and in ways that were highly unique, exciting, and provided loads of room for expansion.

And the best part, I would be spending my days doing the things I love most in the world.

I felt as though I'd been handed the biggest gifts from the universe. But in reality, they were gifts I'd had all along. Just like Dorothy discovered with her beautiful red shoes, all I needed to do was use them—and I came home to my Self.

Liberty Forrest
Speaker, Author and Intuitive Mentor
www.libertyforrest.com

Simply Fearless Love

For me being a woman entrepreneur over 50 is about using my gifts in service to God/dess and all life. From the vantage point of 63, I see how God/dess has been preparing me all my life to start my current business. There's been an intimate dance between my professional/business and spiritual development, and over time, they have become so intertwined as to be inseparable.

Over my 30+ year career as training and development professional, my all-time favorite project was training facilitators to lead diversity workshops with volunteer leaders at AARP in Washington, DC. There was remarkable wisdom in that team: one was a Japanese-American woman who was incarcerated with her family in an internment camp during WWII; another was a Potawatomi medicine man; still another was a white principal of an all-black elementary school in Georgia when it was integrated, literally overnight. As we shared our stories, we created a sacred container of trust and safety to explore our own prejudices and the effects of institutional racism. A great deal of spiritual pain was witnessed and healed in that circle, bringing spirituality into my professional life.

This next story starts in the spiritual: coming out as lesbian at the ripe old age of 38 led me to the Metropolitan Community Church in DC, a denomination ministering particularly to GLBTQ people. My previous churches had been more head-based than heart-based, and worship had been a largely intellectual exercise. At MCC-DC, I experienced God/dess' love for me as an individual, and began developing a deeply intimate relationship of trust with Her.

A couple of years into my time at MCC-DC, I was laid off from AARP with a year's severance pay. My plan was to start my own consulting practice, and my newfound relationship with Spirit allowed me to listen consciously for Divine guidance. It turned out that God/dess' plan for me was to do a Master's program in Culture and Spirituality at the Sophia Center in Oakland, CA, so I packed up and moved across the country. It was a powerful lesson in trusting that Spirit has a far larger view of what's in my best interest than I do.

In one of my classes at the Sophia Center, we were assigned to read *When God Was a Woman,* by Merlin Stone. I was astonished—I had never seen anything but masculine images of the Divine. I was transfixed to discover the Goddess within and learn to express Her power and wisdom in my own life, setting me on the path to becoming a Wiccan priestess. Leading ritual is all about sensing and directing energy—so my priestess years were intense training in allowing God/dess to have Her way.

That experience of getting to know the Divine Feminine also led to my first business, ReMembering Her, helping women reconnect with the grace and power of the Divine Feminine through nature, creativity and the body. Sadly, I fell into the trap of thinking I knew what I needed to be a business owner because of my vast expertise as a trainer, when in fact I had no idea how to market myself. After skimping by for two years, I went back to a j-o-b facilitating workshop.

Spirit's gift to me in that job was discovering a revolutionary new approach to organizational change, shifting from figuring out what's wrong and fixing it, to looking for what's working well and spreading those best practices. This positive focus integrated perfectly with my Wiccan practice, so I put it all together in my second business, Inspiring Results, offering strengths-based consulting and training to non-profits.

When Inspiring Results took me to Santa Cruz, CA on contract, I found myself drawn powerfully to a New Thought spiritual community called Inner Light Ministries. I immediately resonated with the philosophy/theology, finding that it integrated my professional experience and spiritual history into a coherent philosophy that really worked for me. I was uplifted by the worship service, inspired by the choir's music and the preaching, and quickly felt at home in the community. I learned practical spiritual tools I applied in my day-to-day life, and found increasing ease, joy, and peace.

I began an intensive four-year training program to become a New Thought Practitioner, someone who makes a commitment to serve God/dess, to be a place and space for the Divine to express in the physical world.

A couple years after I'd completed the practitioner program, I received the most shocking phone call of my life; my mom had been diagnosed with an aggressive form of lung cancer and likely wouldn't live more than 3 or 4 months. There had been no warning signs at all, and I was dumbfounded. As adults, my mom and I had developed a profound spiritual connection, and loved each other deeply. I knew instantly that all I wanted was to spend whatever time she had left with her and my dad. I packed up my life in Santa Cruz as best I could and was on a plane the next day.

In a conversation two days after her diagnosis, Mom said to me, "I've been thinking about the adventure I'm going on, and wondering what it will be like." In her last months, I witnessed her consciously prepare to leave this world and move on to the next. It was simultaneously the biggest tragedy and the biggest gift of my life, and it was my practitioner training that made it possible to be a loving presence for her. I both discovered and cultivated my capacity for what I came to call "simply fearless love" during that time.

Simply fearless love has become the foundation for my life and now for my third business, Our Climate Change Legacy, with a mission of unleashing the fierce love, wisdom, and power of a million elders to turn the tide on climate change.

Do you see how the threads have woven together? This is what makes me say that God/dess has been preparing me my whole life for this work.

Nancy Ogilvie
Workshops, presentations and a membership community, Our Climate Change Legacy, based in Ann Arbor, MI USA. www.ourcclegacy.net; ourcclegacy@gmail.com.

Take a Step

Hi, my name is Patricia and I live in Cambridgeshire, England. I'm in my late 60s. I've undertaken several types of work earlier in my life. I've been a typist, a Social Worker, and when I was at college I did all sorts of odd jobs—driving a van, working in a pub kitchen, cleaning, waitressing, and others long forgotten. But for about twenty five years I enjoyed working as a freelance training consultant, tutoring on courses for leadership and communication skills.

In 1995 my husband and I immigrated to Sydney, Australia. It was a trial period. We got extendable two year visas and kept our home in the UK in case we didn't settle. Shortly after he started his new job my husband began an affair with a colleague and we split up.

I returned to England after just six months, devastated. I also slipped a disc in my back and was in constant pain.

Luckily I was able to pick up with my old training clients, but after selling the family home and buying one for myself I took a long hard look at my finances. I was 48, and retirement suddenly seemed not so far away. I'd had relatively few years in a pension scheme because I'd only worked part time to fit in with my family's needs. I'd get my state pension when I was 60, but who would want to try to live on that?

My soon-to-be ex-husband was ten years younger so I couldn't claim on his pension until he was at least 65 and I was 75. Things looked bleak for my long term future. I realised that I needed to make more money to secure my retirement.

I'd like to say I developed a plan, but that would be untrue. What is true is that my ears and my mind were open to ideas and opportunities. I've always believed that what you are alert to, you notice, even if at another time it might be invisible to you.

Not long after, a chance comment changed everything. That comment was "I hear it's easy these days to borrow money to buy houses." This was before buy-to-let was even heard of and I had no idea how to set about borrowing money. After all, I already had a home and a mortgage. I was 49 by then. Who would lend money to me?

I phoned an Estate Agent and asked their advice, expecting them to laugh at my ignorance. The guy politely asked me a few questions and told me how to finance another property.

Within three months I had bought three flats and thoroughly frightened myself. I was in a lot of debt, but most would be covered by the rents. Not all though. I knew I'd have to make up the difference and pay for repairs, allow for voids and all the other incidental but not inconsiderable costs.

Gulp!

I've always thought that on my gravestone I'd be happy if someone put "She was kind, she helped people." Being a landlady might seem against that, but I'm a good landlady and wouldn't let out anywhere I wouldn't live in myself. I've always had reasonable organisational and financial skills and put those to good use in this new role in life. But boy, it was scary for a while. My daughters were busy with their own lives and I had to make all the decisions myself from what property to buy to what type of kitchen units to put in. I was on a steep learning curve, but they've never frightened me. I love learning.

I had a lot of support from great friends but they couldn't make these tough decisions for me. Nonetheless I valued every conversation with them. They were very supportive.

Three years later I put an ad in a Lonely Hearts column and met Rick, my "new" husband. In fact, I advertised for three years before I found my new soul-mate. By then I was 51 and he was 48. Who said that men always want younger women? In that three years I had met many available men my own age. So if you're looking for a new partner don't let being of menopausal age put you off. I've always remembered a phrase, "Fish where the fishes are." Get great support from your women friends, but get out there and meet men. Join clubs, use Internet dating sites, use newspaper ads. Those guys won't come knocking on your door if they don't know you exist. And I'll tell you a secret—during those three years I dated FIFTY men, most of them only once. So never give up! And of course the same is true if you're looking for a new special woman in your life.

But back to my business. Rick joined me in the property buying and we decided to make property investment more of a full-time job. By then buy-to-let mortgages were easy to get, and property prices were in a slump. We went on a spending spree and got up to fourteen properties. We have the same attitude to our business. We only buy attractive properties and keep them well-maintained.

The most important action I took to start the business was simple—I stopped thinking about it and did something. It was a small step—just a phone call. I find that so often if I'm hesitating to make a decision, it's because I don't have enough information. If you're thinking about becoming a new, midlife entrepreneur don't let anything stop you. Get all the information you can, weigh up the risks and benefits, take advice from relevant people and if the signs look good, what are you waiting for?

Make a start. Do you really want to be sitting there in ten years' time, ten years older, looking back and regretting what you didn't do?

Patricia McBride
Author, Property Owner, and Therapist
http://stressandphobiasolutions.com/

Follow Your Heart and Dance With Life

I think I got my entrepreneurial spirit from my dad. He was a teacher who also started a trailer sales business in his early forties. Dad was achievement oriented and encouraged me to strive for excellence in all I did. Mum was really supportive.

When I left school I wanted to start earning a living to support myself as quickly as possible. I had a strong desire to make a difference and to help disadvantaged groups. Training to be a nurse seemed to be a natural choice and the training program was not very long. After graduating I worked in cardiology, mental health, and in community health nursing.

I have always loved to study and learn so my next step was to go to graduate school so that I could teach nursing. My husband was a Brit and I went to University in Scotland. I discovered that I loved teaching, designing courses, and curricula and doing research to better understand others. Following graduate school I taught nursing for five years at 2 Canadian universities.

From there I worked for the regional and then the federal government in Ottawa as a Health Promotion Consultant. My husband got a job in Colombia and I took our 2 children then 3 and 5 to live in a small village in the mountains of northern Colombia. During that time I designed and implemented a health promotion project with a peasant farmer organization as a volunteer. Later I was commissioned by the Pan American Health Organisation to write a document, "Health Promotion: Improving the Health Status of Women and Promoting Equality." I was privileged to work for the World Health Organisation as a delegate to Russia just after "the wall" came down and later in Poland.

I was lured away from public service by the partner in a process/management consulting company who spotted my skills in facilitation in a course he was teaching that I participated in. After 6 months, I set up my own process management and consulting company and never looked back. I had a lot of contacts in the health sector and was soon being asked to design and facilitate workshops and do qualitative studies for a number of health-related organizations and government departments. Within two years of starting my own business, I was making six figures.

I love to travel and I had always wanted to do international work but it was not practical while my children were young and my husband was working away a lot. In 2003 a friend connected me with the VP of an international development consulting company and I was invited to manage a large project in Pakistan. After three months I was invited to join full-time and moved to their headquarters in Calgary. Around that time my son was starting University and, after some soul searching, I separated from my husband.

In the following years I managed multi-million dollar projects in Pakistan and Nigeria to build capacity, partnerships, and infrastructure in the health sector, work that I very much enjoyed and am proud of. Then due to budget cuts on the project I was working on, I felt it was time to move on again. I was living in Calgary, a long way from my Ottawa connections and friends and returned to doing domestic consulting/ my own business.

In 2008 I moved to British Columbia with my new partner. I was drawn to training to be a coach and applied my diverse background and experience to this new profession. After studying life and business coaching at Leadership University, I founded the Creative Healing Centre where coaching, healing, and the arts came together. I set up a network of coaches to help people through various life transitions such as in work and in relationships. I was enjoying the work but soon knew I wanted to reach more people than I could through one-to-one coaching. I wanted to make a bigger difference—faster!

I put these thoughts out there and shortly thereafter was offered the opportunity to work as a Senior Technical Advisor to the Ministry of Public Health in Afghanistan. I went to live in Kabul for thirteen months at a dangerous time when there were frequent suicide bombings. It was rewarding work and I was sorry to leave there. I carried on supporting the team virtually for 6 months after. Within a few weeks of returning home, I was approached by the VP of a not-for- profit organization that promotes women's and children's rights around the world. I felt aligned with their mission and values and before long was hired on contract as a Senior Health Advisor on 7 projects in Asia and Africa to reduce infant and maternal mortality.

In late 2012 I came close to burning out after pushing my body for so many years. I decided to finally listen to my body's wisdom and take some time out. I wanted to create more balance in my life and started 2013 with little structure. I took a program on mindfulness, slept, and re-connected with family and friends. My moment of epiphany came while doing a guided mediation. I had a sudden image of a globe with interconnected points of light coming on all around it. I interpreted this to be women lighting up/ becoming conscious around the world and realized that my purpose was "To help build peace in the world, one woman at a time."

From that came my new enterprise, the Creative Living Community, and coaching women individually and in groups to transform their lives from constantly striving and driving to healthy balanced lives of fun, fulfilment, passion, and inner peace. In 2016 I launched my book *Learning to Dance with Life; A* Guide for High Achieving Women which reached #1 international best seller on Amazon. I'm passionate about helping women to find peace amidst the chaos of daily life and work. Through helping women they can then help build peace in their families, workplaces, and communities.

I work with women one-to-one and in groups, face-to-face and virtually. I love public speaking so that I can get my message out to a wider audience and inspire others.

Through this amazing life journey so far I have stayed true to my values: contribution, love of learning, connection, adventure, and freedom. I know that I don't do well in structures so setting up my own businesses has been a good fit for me.

I am grateful to my parents for helping me believe that I can do anything I set my mind to.

Success for me now is about living my life in alignment with my core values. My mother died from breast cancer at the age of 62 and that inspired me to do personal growth work and to continually learn and grow.

My top tips for women making the move into midlife entrepreneurship are to clarify your core values, and live in alignment with them; listen to your body's wisdom and follow your heart.

———————————

Pamela Thompson
Author, <u>Learning to Dance with Life:</u> A Guide for High Achieving Women
President and CEO, Creative Life Coaching Inc. & Founder, Creative Living Community
http://www.creativelivingcommunity.com

The Entrepreneurial Spirit Requires Re-inventing Yourself

Whoa! It's been quite a ride so far, and I'm a long way from done! Life gets more focused, more expansive, and more interesting with every day.

High school was a breeze. The future looked bright. As I was finishing my pre-med college days, the unthinkable happened. I was pregnant. At that time, to my parents and my world, it was a shocking admission of immoral choices with damning consequences. For me, it was just "Next!"

I finished the year at college, huge, and happy, followed by a month in a hospital on bedrest, due to toxaemia. That provided a great time to collect my thoughts, and make plans, the first of which was to get as far away from the parents as possible, and have my baby in peace.

A new mother, without support of any kind from the parents, I had to make it happen. I worked at administrative jobs until I could return to college. I felt medicine was out of the question with a small child. Too many long hours and uncertain schedules!

Education seemed a sensible career option for one with a child, so I studied educational psychology and got a teaching credential. I married had two more children, and ended up with three children . . . and alone, again. So glad my foresight had created a secure job with benefits!

Teaching was not enough. I finished my Master's and PhD in Psychology on weekends, summers, and in stolen moments when children were sleeping and I was not working.

I produced full-scale musicals, became the president of anything that interested me, and wrote books, created products, and spoke at major conferences on weekends. That's how I survived because teaching held no challenges, and the politics of it were depressing.

All through this amazingly tedious work life, I promised myself that, when my last child had been on his own for two years, I could quit and live the entrepreneurial life full out. I did that. I left the confines of a life that held me down, moved from Canada to San Diego, CA, and became a full-time speaker, author, and relationship expert.

What a shift! Now, I was responsible for every single thing that could keep me fed: content, marketing, promotion, networking, product development, sales, negotiation, and, of course, seeing my clients. And, all that in a new country with no connections or friends! It was exciting, stimulating, and downright scary.

I knew I could do it. Everyone I left behind thought I had lost my mind.

Why was I so sure? Because I know I have the power and ability to re-invent myself in dire circumstances. That's important for everyone, but it is an entrepreneurial necessity!

I had a purpose then: It was to help people play nicely together at home and at work. I jumped in, found ways to reach training managers and meeting planners, and made my way as a road warrior, speaking and consulting. I wrote a few books, and learned how to let the world know. Easy? Hell, no! What a learning curve!

There were times that I walked on the edge, having to talk someone into hiring me if I wanted to keep eating. There were times I celebrated when a plan came together. And, there was everything in between.

People were disappointing. I believed in collaboration. They quickly demonstrated competition. I believed in giving, they, in getting. They didn't keep their word, misrepresented themselves, and lead me to dead ends. But, that's on them. I just kept on turning over rocks until I found the gold.

Fortunately, I held on to one belief: Go within when you're without!

Be still. Dig deep. Listen well. Walk on when clear. Correct course when needed. (. . . and, if required, use credit cards and eat Ramen to live your purpose and make your contribution!)

In the last fifteen years in San Diego, my purpose has evolved, narrowed, and deepened: I work with the partners, ex's, families, and co-workers of chronically difficult people, worldwide. I help them to understand the patterns and strategically escape from them. My ulterior mission is to be a voice for the children caught within dysfunctional spousal relationships by working with their parents.

My sixteenth book was just released, and that is always exciting. Writing is a major way of connecting with the world for me. Syndicated globally, it's my way of reaching out.

Success to me is living a healthy life while optimizing my contribution to my niche. Balance is key. So many of my long-time friends repeatedly ask me if, and when, I might retire. My answer is always the same:

"My definition of retirement is having the luxury to do exactly what I want to do all day. I'm doing it, therefore, I must be retired!"

And, on a more serious note, I'm with Steve Jobs: "Your work is going to fill a large part of your life, and the only way to be truly satisfied is to do what you believe is great work. And, the only way to do great work is to love what you do. If you haven't found it yet, keep looking. Don't settle. As with all matters of the heart, you'll know when you find it."

I've found it and refined it. Now, I know exactly what to do each day, and I look forward to it. I love it. And, therefore, it is attractive.

Having an amazing tribe of fellow entrepreneurs who are gentle, generous, loving, and collaborative is important. It took kissing a few toads to find them, but I persevered. When one group isn't right for you, carry on. It's worth it to find that tribe!

People may question your sanity, put you down for taking risks, and try to talk you out of what you know is right for you. Love them. Bless them. Move on.

There is passion in purpose, and when you find yours, be unstoppable!

Rhoberta Shaler, PhD
The Relationship Help Doctor, offers urgent and ongoing care for individuals, couples and companies globally. Her ebook series, Escaping the Hijackal Trap*: The Definitive Guide to Dealing with Chronically Difficult People, launched in 2016.*
www.ForRelationshipHelp.com
www.Hijackals.com

Just One Regret . . . Maybe?

"I really need you now!" demanded my father. Were they the 5 words I would live to regret?

It was Easter 1977, I was 16 years old and busy revising for my exams. My father wanted me to leave school there and then, to go and work for him. "You don't need qualifications, just common sense!" he cried.

Maybe he was right. Revise or earn money? It was too tempting, I chose the latter. I left school without a qualification to my name, with some extremely angry teachers and a very upset mother.

For the next 10 years I worked on a market stall in London selling car accessories! Driving a van that I unloaded and loaded every single day!

I think it was in year 7 that I realised I would go crazy if I didn't do something else a little more mentally stimulating. But what could I do? I had no qualifications which as a result left me with little confidence; the thought of writing a job application filled me with dread!

So I stayed on the markets and started to expand. I bought a couple more stalls and employed staff to work on them for me. I had friends in the fashion industry, so I bought their surplus stock (or cabbage as it was called in the trade!), a friend with a petrol station who sold me his promotional stock, and anything else I could find for a good price, from gardening implements to hardware.

The money was flowing in but I was unhappy, I needed a "real" challenge. I couldn't bear to think that I could spend the rest of my life arguing over who was going to get their van in first, or how business wasn't so good because of the weather.

In May 1987 I met Steven, my husband-to-be. He was the manager of a really lovely restaurant and hotel called The White Hart. He had spent the last year looking for a restaurant to buy, but he needed a business partner. I had only known Steven three weeks when we went to look at restaurant with the view to purchase.

As we arrived, I was mesmerised by the most beautiful pink, thatched restaurant called The Pink Geranium. When we drove up the drive I could feel myself smiling, in fact I could not stop myself from smiling the whole time we were there. I had fallen in love; nothing was going to stop me from owning The Pink Geranium.

Come September 1st 1987, I was now the proud owner of the most beautiful restaurant in the world.

I remember my first few weeks there at The Pink Geranium, I was so nervous that I had to have several G&Ts before I could meet our guests! They all seemed so educated and spoke so well. After all, what did I know? I was just an East End girl who couldn't string a grammatically correct sentence together? Then I realised that it didn't matter how well they spoke or how educated they were, that we were basically all the same with similar insecurities.

During the following 10 years, business was thriving. I became the proud mother of two lovely daughters, Serena and Stefanie, and had purchased another equally beautiful restaurant and hotel called The Sheene Mill.

By 2003 my life was not so good, my marriage was on the rocks, I was 43 and felt like I still hadn't achieved something in my own right, and still hadn't satisfied my soul. I was back to my same old story; I had no qualifications and little confidence.

Opposite to The Sheene Mill a building had been put up for sale. It was an old timber framed building that used to be an engineering works. Somehow I knew I had to buy it, although at that time I didn't have the faintest idea what I should do with it.

I had always been passionate about health, beauty, and fashion and believe that I have an instinctive knowing of what people "need" and want. I put that down to having mixed with people from lots of different "walks of life."

I decided to create a place that would combine all of my passions. A ladies clothing boutique with a coffee/champagne bar in the centre, four beauty treatment rooms, and a small area for exercise.

I still had doubts that "retail" wouldn't satisfy my soul, but it felt right, so I went with it.

Shortly after opening there were two things that happened that made me realise my destiny;

1. A lady in her 50s came into my shop; I could see/feel how she lacked in self-esteem. She opened up to me, and explained that her husband had just left her and that she needed help to get her life back together again.

I recommended an eyebrow shape, that's all! She left feeling stronger and much happier.

2. I was interviewing a bereavement councillor with the view to rent one of my rooms and as I listened to how she had been helping others, I started to cry.

It then dawned on me, that my purpose in life is to help people; whether it is just an eyebrow shape, a new outfit, to lose weight, to eat more healthily, to get more fit, or just to lend an "ear" over a cup of coffee. My little shop, ESSE, was to become an escape, a haven for people to come to, when in need of some TLC.

I followed my passion and, as always, my gut instinct. Rumours that ESSE wouldn't work (due to it being in the middle of nowhere!) only made me more determined, I fought with vengeance, working in excess of 80 hours.

11 years later . . . 6 treatment rooms, 2 exercise studios, a thriving boutique, thousands of friends/clients and a new and very lovely husband named Ollie.

Just one regret? No, never, I have always believed in life that one thing always leads to another. Just stay "open" and ready to receive what life puts in front of you, allowing yourself be taken on the most wonderful journey.

I believe that there is no happier person than a person whose job is their hobby!

Sally Saunders-Makings
Proprietor of ESSE Retail and Therapy and The Sheene Mill Hotel and Restaurant.
http://www.esse.uk.com/
http://thesheenemill.com/

Dancing with Life Again!

I was raised on a farm where every day was a struggle just to put food on the table. All I knew was work and loneliness. The animals came first for our survival. My father wanted sons but instead had 4 daughters and one son that lived. The last baby born was a boy that died at birth and my father was devastated.

During my early school years I needed help with speaking and I was pulled out of class for extra assistance which began my isolation and feeling of being not quite right compared to the other children. I worked hard to fit in but that caused a bigger problem for me. Even though I had three sisters of my own, the eldest was already busy with life itself and the two closest to me hated just hearing my name—yet they did not know me as a person—as it was always Wendy did this, Wendy did that by my father which separated us completely. Our connection was lost.

Being raised on a farm was not all bad as I enjoyed watching new life come into being, so tiny, helpless and yet warm and loving and I enjoyed their companionship. However, I would wake up one morning only to discover that they were gone, setting a belief within me that what I loved would never last and be taken from me.

At the age of 9 my father and brother were standing in the middle of the yard and dad was telling my brother how all this would be his one day and I looked up at him and said, "But, Dad, what about me?" He looked down and replied, "But you're just a girl." That day I lost my sense of self-worth completely and my voice. I never did have a girlfriend that I could call my best friend to share things with. Our farm was surrounded by a seven foot fence to keep the animals in—but it also kept the world out.

During my high school years I was like a ghost travelling down the corridors just going through the motions. One day, I saw an ad that guaranteed me a government job with great income and I knew deep down within my core that I did not want my children, if I had any, to live in poverty, so I jumped at the opportunity—although English was not my best subject, I was committed to being more for them.

After graduating it was no surprise, though, that I had married the first man who gave me any attention as I remember saying to myself, "Who would want me!" I can still hear those words as if it were yesterday inside my head. That began a 25 year verbally abusive marriage. It was only when the pain became too much to bear, did I finally find it within myself to say, "You don't deserve to be treated like this! Wendy, stand up for yourself!" And when I did, my children said, "Mum, what took you so long?" I thought I was hiding my pain from them, yet all that time I was only fooling myself.

I then began a new journey of rebuilding my life from scratch while caring for those who counted on me most to be strong: my children, my mother, and my staff.

For six years I worked long and hard and cried myself to sleep many nights, praying to find a man that had three qualities:

1. Slow to anger

2. A Giver not a taker and

3. Could love me as much as I could love him.

Although I never believed I would find him—I did. In 2009 Carmon and I were married on Valentine's Day with our now combined families, 6 children and 13 grandchildren, in our home in front of our fireplace. I picked Valentine's Day as I thought, wow, each year I would get two gifts instead of one and he could never forget that date. LOL.

Two months after the happiest day of my life, Carmon and I were sitting in the doctor's office as we were advised that Carmon had 3rd stage colon cancer. I couldn't believe what I was hearing. I dropped everything I was doing and began to research ways to try and save the love of my life, Carmon.

Over the next 6 years Carmon and I fought his battle together and each time when we thought we had it beat, the cancer would come back. It was when we received the news that the cancer had jumped to his liver that I felt totally devastated. It felt like when I took two steps forward, I was taking ten back. I was lost and hit bottom. It was only then, again, when the pain was too great to bear alone, that I reached out and discovered a community of women that provided me with the strength, support, love, and tools to carry me through this journey and onward to my passion today.

By November 11, 2011 my life had been transformed so much that it created a yearning inside me to give back. "Don't keep this to yourself", I wanted to shout from the rooftops, "Life doesn't have to be this hard, and you are not alone!" So when my community of BraveHeart Women asked for women to come forward to help launch BraveHeart Women in our local communities, I jumped at the opportunity.

Then fear set in. I had never spoken to a group of people in my life—what was I thinking! But my soul wouldn't let me quit on myself this time and I remained open and over the next few years, invested in myself with mentors and courses and I continually evolved.

On December 7th, 2014 Carmon transitioned in our home in front of the exact fireplace where we had just six years earlier exchanged our wedding vows, surrounded by our children and now 15 grandchildren.

I now know that everything in my life happened for a reason and guided me to where I am today and I am truly thankful for all of my experiences. My 40 years as a court reporter gave me the opportunity to not only listen but I viscerally felt the pain of women from all walks of life and all ages share their stories, hear their cries of loneliness, and feelings of worthlessness.

While at the same time, I watched communities come together in times of devastation such as SARS and Walkerton, and find within themselves the strength to support each other while grieving and ensure that the disaster did not repeat itself again—to save others heartache.

This is WHY I do what I do. I want to bring women together in Community and guide them out of pain, support them like a sister and ensure they never feel alone again. I have been able to take my life experiences, many years of loneliness, lack of self-worth and support, and turn it into a beautiful community of Oneness.

And, that assists me and keeps me motivated each day to embrace other women that may be where I once was and that if she is open, she can learn to dance with life again, find joy in her heart, and friendships that last a lifetime with US.

Wendy Woodworth
A Guide by Your Side
www.WendyWoodworth.com

REFERENCES

Covey, Stephen, R. *The 7 Habits of Highly Effective People*, 1989

Dilts, R. *Next Generation Entrepreneurs*, 2015, Dilts Strategy Group

Dilts, R. & DeLozier, J. *Encyclopedia of Systemic NLP and NLP Coding*, http://nlpuniversitypress.com/

Equality & Human Rights Commission 2010 Working Better, Introduction

Godin, S., *Tribes: We need you to lead us*, 2008, Piatkus Books

Kauffman Index of Entrepreneurial Activity, 1996-2008

Lazarus, J., Successful NLP; For the results you want. 2010, Crimson Publishing

McKenna, P. Change Your Life in 7 Days, 2004, Bantam Press

Sinek, S. *Start with Why*, 2009, Portfolio Penguin

http://www.telegraph.co.uk/sponsored/business/volvo-business/focus-on/11902855/rise-of-the-older-preneurs.html

http://www.viacharacter.org/www/Character-Strengths

Resources for Midlife Entrepreneurs

https://www.sba.gov/content/50-entrepreneurs

http://seniorentrepreneurshipworks.org/about.php

http://takecommand.org/

http://www.entrepreneur.com/

Personality Tests

Myers Briggs http://www.myersbriggs.org/my-mbti-personality-type/take-the-mbti-instrument/

Big Five http://www.outofservice.com/bigfive/info/

Enneagram http://www.enneagramtest.net/

Character Strengths https://www.authentichappiness.sas.upenn.edu/ Go to "Questionnaires" and select "VIA Survey of Character Strengths"

Outsource Links

Elance https://www.elance.com/

Fiverr https://www.fiverr.com/

Five Squid https://www.fivesquid.com/

Freelancer https://www.freelancer.co.uk/

Upwork https://www.upwork.com/

Elevator Pitch

https://www.mindtools.com/pages/article/elevator-pitch.htm

Business Plans

Business in a Box http://www.business-in-a-box.com/

Law Depot http://www.lawdepot.co.uk/

Gov.uk https://www.gov.uk/write-business-plan

Bplans http://www.bplans.com/services_business_plan_templates.php

Time Management

Gantt http://www.ganttexcel.com/

Gantt https://www.smartdraw.com/gantt-chart/

Time Management for the Office http://www.amazon.co.uk/Time-Management-Office-Patricia-McBride-ebook/dp/B00ASC7V0M/ref=sr_1_4?ie=UTF8&qid=1458398944&sr=8-4&keywords=patricia+mcbride

Other Resources

Setting up a Mastermind Group http://www.lifehack.org/articles/featured/how-to-start-and-run-a-mastermind-group.html

Reasons to join a Mastermind Group http://www.forbes.com/sites/chicceo/2013/10/21/7-reasons-to-join-a-mastermind-group/#3de3c6a817ab

*Mass Influence:*The Habits of the Highly Influential, 2015, Teresa de Grosbois with Karen Rowe, Wildfire

GPS Your Best Life: Charting Your Destination and Getting There in Style, 2012, Charmaine Hammond

Happy for No Reason: 7 Steps to Being Happy from the Inside Out, 2009, Marci Shimoff

ALSO BY PAT DUCKWORTH

Available on Amazon and your local bookstore.

 ## Hot Women Cool Solutions

How to control menopause symptoms using mind/body techniques, 2012

 ## How to Survive Her Menopause

2013

 ## Cool Recipes for Hot Women

2014

Co-Authored Books

The Hypnotherapy Handbook

with Ann Jaloba and others, 2014

Your 101 Ways to 101

with Dr George Grant, 2013

Away From Home

The Planet of Wellness with Marina
Nani and others, 2013

Chocolate and Diamonds for the Woman's Soul

with Carla Wynn Hall and
others, 2015